Las Vegas

DIRECTIONS

D0465320

WRITTEN AND RESEARCHED BY

Greg Ward

ROUGH GUIDES

NEW YORK • LONDON • DELHI

www.roughguides.com

Contents

Introduction to

Las Vegas

▲ Binion's Horseshoe casino

Shimmering from the desert haze of Nevada like a latter-day El Dorado, Las Vegas is the most dynamic, spectacular city on earth. At the start of the twentieth century, it didn't even exist; a hundred years on, it's home to well over one million people, and still growing fast.

Las Vegas is not like other popular destinations: the tourists haven't spoiled the "real" city; there is no real city. With no sense of history or fascinating neighborhoods to explore, the whole thing is completely self-referential; the reason Las Vegas boasts the vast majority of the world's largest hotels is that thirty-seven million tourists each year come just to see the hotels themselves.

The basic concept of the Strip hotel/casino has been endlessly refined, from the Western-themed resorts and ranches of the 1940s, via a trend for Disney-esque fantasy that started in the late 1960s with Caesars Palace and culminated with Excalibur and Luxor in the early 1990s, to today's hyperactive quest for novelty. Long before

When to visit

Las Vegas is at the heart of the hottest, harshest **desert** in North America, and so receives less than four inches of rain (10cm) per year. Temperatures, however, vary enormously, with daytime maximums averaging over **100°F** (38°C) in July and August, and night-time minimums dropping below **freezing** in December and January. As the cliché goes, at least it's a dry heat, meaning that the lack of humidity often makes things more pleasant than they should be. That said, the **mid-summer** heat on the Strip is quite unbearable, making it impossible to walk any distance during the day, so the ideal times to visit are in **spring** between April and May and also during **fall** between September and October. Note that hotel swimming pools tend to be closed between October and March inclusive.

The city is at its quietest, and room rates are therefore lowest, during the first few weeks of December and the last few weeks of January, and also during June and July, while Christmas and New Year are the busiest periods of all.

▲ The Venetian's Grand Canal

they lose their sparkle, yesterday's showpieces are blasted into rubble, to make way for ever more extravagant replacements.

In addition to providing eye-pleasing spectacles, Las Vegas is a city that makes a point of catering to visitors. If you come in search of the cheapest destination in America, you'll enjoy paying rock-bottom rates for accommodation and hunting out buffet bargains. If it's style and opulence you're after, you can dine in the finest restaurants, shop in the chicest stores, and watch world-class entertainment; it'll cost you, but not as much as it would anywhere else. The same goes for gambling. The Strip giants cater to those who want sophisticated high-roller heavens; if you prefer your casinos sinful and seedy, there's no shortage of that kind either, especially downtown.

◀ The Bellagio

On the face of it, the city is supremely democratic – you'll be welcomed everywhere, no matter how you look – but all that seductive deference comes

▲ Slot machines

at a price. Ninety percent of visitors gamble, losing on average over $500 each. What's so clever about Las Vegas is that it makes absolutely certain that you have such a good time that you don't mind losing a bit of money along the way; that's why they don't even call it "gambling" anymore, but "gaming."

▼ The Stratosphere

Las Vegas
AT A GLANCE

The Strip

Las Vegas's fabulous Strip is a true wonder of the world – and features most of the world's other wonders along its four-mile length into the bargain.

The Desert

A few minutes' drive in any direction can take you away from the mayhem of the city into the magnificent, timeless desolation of the Southwestern deserts – and the Grand Canyon is just a short flight away.

▲ Gambling

Gambling

Offering untold riches at the touch of a button or the turn of a card, Las Vegas remains effortlessly ahead of the competition as the best place to gamble on Earth.

▲ Red Rock Canyon

◄ The Strip at night

▲ Cravings Buffet, Mirage

Buffets

You can still pile 'em high for just a few dollars, but these days Las Vegas's finest buffets offer truly excellent food, and attract just as many gourmets as gluttons.

Shows

Thanks largely to the extraordinary success of the Cirque du Soleil, Las Vegas has re-established itself as the entertainment capital of the world – prepare to have your breath taken away by the sheer spectacle of it all.

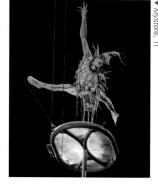

◄ Mystère, TI

Ideas

The big six

In Las Vegas, a city consecrated to the new, there's always some freshly constructed, mind-boggling, man-made marvel clamoring for your attention, and it's inevitably a casino. Ever since the Hoover Dam kick-started the development of the city back in the 1930s, it's been an unending competition to make sure that each new casino is bigger and better than last.

▲ The Venetian

Opulent enough for any high-roller while also still fun for the family, festooned with frescos and echoing to the song of the gondoliers, the city's premier casino epitomizes modern Las Vegas.

P.82 ▸ THE CENTRAL STRIP

▲ The Forum

America's most profitable shopping mall is itself a jaw-dropping virtual-reality experience stuffed inside the faux Roman pomp of Caesars Palace – though the price tags are real enough.

P.97 ▸ THE CENTRAL STRIP

▶ Hoover Dam

A thirty-mile drive out of the city leads to the architectural showpiece that made the whole thing possible, a mighty wall of concrete holding back the Colorado River at the Arizona state line.

P.148 ▶ DAY TRIPS

▼ New York–New York

Whether staying at the hotel or simply dropping in, the gleeful, meticulous styling of this replica Manhattan ensures you'll get a perfect taste of the Big Apple in the desert.

P.57 ▶ THE SOUTH STRIP

▲ Luxor

Fronted by sphinxes and topped by a massive laser beam, this stunning black-glass pyramid abounds with enjoyable ancient-Egyptian imagery inside and out – and ranks among the city's best-value places to stay.

P.54 ▶ THE SOUTH STRIP

▶ Bellagio

If you're looking to live it up in style – with refined restaurants, top-quality entertainment and plush service – look no further than this marble Italianate extravaganza with its own eight-acre lake in front.

P.75 ▶ THE CENTRAL STRIP

Buffets

All-you-can-eat buffets remain a defining feature of almost all Las Vegas casinos. When it's good, the traditional, bargain buffet experience is like having unrestricted access to an upmarket mall's food court: good fast food, but not great cooking. Recent years have seen a new development, however, in which high-end casinos have raised buffet prices to a level that makes it possible to provide feasts fit for true gourmands.

▼ Festival Market Buffet

The Palms, an otherwise upscale new casino, draws an enthusiastic local crowd with its well-priced traditional buffet.

P.129 › WEST OF THE STRIP

▼ The Buffet, Bellagio

Bellagio's sumptuous buffet is the one that set a new agenda for the all-you-can-eat market, providing a gourmet feast in which you never know what to expect next.

P.90 › THE CENTRAL STRIP

▼ Feast Around The World

Sunset Station offers something for everyone at this quintessential locals buffet, which caters to locals looking for decent food from all over the world, at very reasonable prices.

P.140 ▸ EAST OF THE STRIP

▲ Le Village

Though Paris's Le Village is less wide-ranging than almost any other Las Vegas buffet, with the whole of French cuisine to choose from, that's unlikely to prove a problem.

P.90 ▸ THE CENTRAL STRIP

▲ Todai Seafood Buffet

Located in the Aladdin, this is one of the city's few independently run buffets and an utterly irresistible destination for lovers of Japanese seafood.

P.91 ▸ THE CENTRAL STRIP

▶ Garden Court Buffet

Downtown's best buffet, at Main Street Station, is pleasant rather than mind-blowing, but it offers excellent value for the money, at lunchtime especially.

P.120 ▸ DOWNTOWN

Gourmet restaurants

Barely ten years ago, received wisdom had it that Las Vegas visitors were not prepared to pay for fine dining. Now, however, with casinos luring culinary superstars from all over America to open Vegas outlets, many tourists come here specifically for the restaurants. It's now possible to make a virtual cook's tour of all the latest trends in American cuisine simply by spending a few nights eating out in Las Vegas.

▲ Nobu

A quietly subdued haven of wonderful, Japanese-influenced cuisine in the otherwise hectic Hard Rock – expensive but well worth it.

P.139 ▸ EAST OF THE STRIP

▼ Olives

Todd English's modern, Italian-themed cooking finds a perfect setting facing the lake at Bellagio – try to get a table outside.

P.88 ▸ THE CENTRAL STRIP

▼ Bouchon

Thomas Keller's French bistro, beautifully located on an elegant upper-story patio at the Venetian, has a menu that's just as ravishing as the decor.

P.84 ▶ THE CENTRAL STRIP

▲ 8-0-8

A sampling of Jean-Marie Josselin's zestful creations provides a perfect little taste of Hawaii, albeit amidst the general post-modern weirdness that is Caesars Palace.

P.84 ▶ THE CENTRAL STRIP

▼ Commander's Palace

Superb traditional Creole cooking from New Orleans (where the original restaurant is a culinary landmark), served in a formal but very friendly atmosphere at the Aladdin.

P.85 ▶ THE CENTRAL STRIP

▲ Aureole

Everyone raves about the wine list – and the eye-catching "wine tower" – at Mandalay Bay's *Aureole*, but the contemporary American food is every bit as impressive.

P.61 ▶ THE SOUTH STRIP

Casual restaurants

Between the two extremes of Las Vegas's restaurant scene – the all-you-can-eat buffet and the no-expense-spared gourmet joints – it's still possible to eat good, well-prepared food, served at reasonable prices in atmospheric surroundings. You can't beat having an open-air lunch right on the Strip, while for breakfast and dinner there's a lot to be said for an old-fashioned casino coffeeshop, with its no-frills service, hefty portions, and hard-bitten clientele.

▲ Mon Ami Gabi

The perfect venue for an alfresco French bistro lunch, on a terrace patio immediately beneath Paris's Eiffel Tower.

P.87 ▶ THE CENTRAL STRIP

▲ Vialé

This spacious open-air Italian restaurant in front of Caesars Palace offers a welcome break for pedestrians trudging along the Strip in the midday sun.

P.89 ▶ THE CENTRAL STRIP

▼ Margarita's Mexican Cantina

Before their design and attractions became more important than the food, gambling or prices, every Las Vegas casino boasted atmospheric and inexpensive eateries like this time capsule at the New Frontier.

P.108 ▶ THE NORTH STRIP

▲ Mr Lucky's 24/7

The Hard Rock hasn't really been in Las Vegas very long, but its 24-hour coffeeshop does a great job of evoking how the city used to be – or perhaps ought to be.

P.138 ▶ EAST OF THE STRIP

▶ Paymon's Mediterranean Café and Market

A true Las Vegas gem, well away from the Strip near the university, and offering the best-value vegetarian food in the city.

P.139 ▶ EAST OF THE STRIP

▼ Binion's Horseshoe Coffee Shop

A true veteran of the downtown scene, for many diners this basement coffeeshop, far removed from the modern Strip in the old-school gambling mecca of Binion's Horseshoe, encapsulates what Las Vegas is all about.

P.119 ▶ DOWNTOWN

Bars and lounges

As the perfect fuel to turn a dithering gawker into a diehard gambler, alcohol is very easy to come by. If you want a drink in a casino, a tray-toting waitress will find you. All the casinos have bars as well, while the old-fashioned Rat-Pack era lounge has returned in force. The booming nightclub scene has seen the emergence of the "ultra-lounge", a high-octane cocktail bar with a dance floor.

▲ Tangerine

Doing a fine job of being all things to all men, this Strip-front "speakeasy" at TI makes a fun stop-off at any hour of the night.

P.92 ▸ THE CENTRAL STRIP

▼ Tabú

MGM Grand plays host to this most lavish and luxurious of Las Vegas's new breed of ultra-lounge, complete with go-go girls and multicolored, touch-sensitive tables.

P.67 ▸ THE SOUTH STRIP

▲ Gaudí Bar

This weirdly undulating mushroom of a bar seems so incongruous out at Sunset Station that after a martini or two you can't help wondering if it's all a hallucination.

P.141 ▸ EAST OF THE STRIP

▼ Ghostbar

With its long-range views of the Strip, this sky-high ultra-lounge at the Palms ranks among the city's most in-demand celebrity hangouts.

P.129 ▸ WEST OF THE STRIP

▲ Quark's Bar

Head here after checking out the Hilton's Star Trek Experience, because how often do you get to wash down unidentifiable alien foodstuffs with bizarre galactic cocktails on the bridge of the *Enterprise*?

P.141 ▸ EAST OF THE STRIP

Clubs

In the new millennium, Las Vegas has finally come of age as an international clubbing capital, with the success of nightclubs at hipper casinos like the Palms and Mandalay Bay prompting their rivals to follow suit, often with spectacular results. More and more tourists are now coming to Las Vegas specifically for the clubs, although it has to be said that it's still somewhat skewed towards older, wealthier customers.

▲ Rain

With its state-of-the-art special effects and stylings, the Palm's showpiece nightspot has become the place to be seen in Las Vegas.

P.130 ▶ WEST OF THE STRIP

▲ Krave

Aladdin's newer, flamboyant nightclub is the Strip's closest approximation to a full-on gay club.

P.92 ▶ THE CENTRAL STRIP

▲ rumjungle

High-energy, eye-popping and extremely hip Latin-flavored nightclub at Mandalay Bay that's a huge hit with twenty-somethings.

P.66 ▸ THE SOUTH STRIP

▼ Risqué

Paris's happy mixture of bar and nightclub attracts an older and slightly more laid-back clientele than its rivals.

P.92 ▸ THE CENTRAL STRIP

▲ Studio 54

This canny evocation of New York's famous disco in the MGM Grand is always dependable for an exciting night on the town.

P.67 ▸ THE SOUTH STRIP

▼ Ra

Everything a Las Vegas nightclub should be – excited crowds, great music, and fabulously camp Egyptian theming.

P.66 ▸ THE SOUTH STRIP

Shows

Las Vegas can still legitimately claim to be the capital of the world's entertainment industry, though it's changed greatly from the days of the Rat Pack. With the major exceptions of Celine Dion and Elton John, who alternate at Caesars Palace, the entertainment scene is dominated less by big-name singers and instead by the postmodern circus/theater troupe, Cirque du Soleil, who currently offer five spectacular permanent productions, with more in the pipeline.

▲ Celine Dion

Caesars Palace's Colosseum makes an amazing venue for a breathtaking big-star show in the great Las Vegas tradition.

P.93 ▸ THE CENTRAL STRIP

▲ O

Utterly amazing Cirque du Soleil production, in an extraordinary theater at Bellagio where the stage repeatedly disappears under water.

P.95 ▸ THE CENTRAL STRIP

▲ Mystère

Las Vegas's original Cirque du Soleil show, still at TI, remains a fabulous and fantastic spectacle – just don't try to figure out what it's about.

P.95 ▸ THE CENTRAL STRIP

▶ The Amazing Johnathan

Low-budget but high-laughter comedy magic with a manic edge that provides one of the only good reasons to go to the Riviera.

P.109 ▸ THE NORTH STRIP

▼ Blue Man Group

This bizarre but compelling blend of performance art, slapstick, and high-octane rock has been a surprisingly durable Vegas success, and with good reason.

P.92 ▸ THE CENTRAL STRIP

Shopping

Before the 1992 unveiling of the Forum at Caesars Palace, none of the casinos had its own shopping mall, and the city's stores catered almost exclusively to locals. Since then, however, malls and arcades have been opening everywhere (there are four top-quality malls on the Strip alone), and an amazing two-thirds of Las Vegas visitors cite shopping as the main reason to come.

▲ Fashion Show Mall

The one mall on the Strip not linked to a casino offers large department stores as well as designer boutiques in a prime location right across from Wynn Las Vegas.

P.110 ▶ THE NORTH STRIP

▲ The Forum Shops

A must-see attraction in its own right, the ever-expanding Forum is bursting with eye-catching stores of all kinds and a batch of fantastic restaurants.

P.97 ▶ THE CENTRAL STRIP

▲ Grand Canal Shoppes

Even more upscale than the Forum, the Venetian's Grand Canal is a great place for window-shopping, and the prices are not always beyond reach.

P.97 ▸ THE CENTRAL STRIP

▲ Desert Passage

Aladdin's mall is less hectic and more spacious than the Forum or Grand Canal, but equally well themed and holding a vast array of distinctive stores.

P.96 ▸ THE CENTRAL STRIP

▲ Mandalay Place

The newest and smallest of the major casino malls has made a determined effort to attract interesting stores not found elsewhere in the city.

P.70 ▸ THE SOUTH STRIP

▲ Las Vegas Outlet Center

It's nothing special to look at, but this sprawling mall south of the Strip is a more likely source of good deals on everyday wear than its big-name rivals.

P.70 ▸ THE SOUTH STRIP

Best places to stay

Because the mega-casinos are the major visitor attractions in Las Vegas, it's easy to forget that they're also hotels as well. Which one you choose to stay in will make a huge difference to your vacation; they're definitely not all the same, and if you end up in one that doesn't suit you, you may feel very stranded indeed.

▲ The Venetian

Luxuriously spacious suites, elite but friendly service, and a great pool area make the Venetian Las Vegas's best upscale option.

P.162 ▶ ACCOMMODATION

▲ Paris

Perfectly positioned at the heart of the Strip (right across from the Bellagio), and imbued with fun French flavor, Paris makes an ideal mid-range alternative.

P.161 ▶ ACCOMMODATION

▲ Circus Circus

Bargain-basement prices and plenty to keep the kids excited; the best choice for an inexpensive family vacation.

▶ New York–New York

With its distinctive Art Deco rooms and surprisingly intimate scale, this mini-Manhattan combines the glamour of a big-name casino with the convenience of a conventional hotel.

◀ Main Street Station

Offering high-standard rooms at appealingly low prices, Main Street Station is downtown's best bargain.

▼ Luxor

What Las Vegas is all about: sleeping for reasonable rates inside a giant Egyptian pyramid with weirdly sloping black-glass walls.

Sim City

While Nevada's casinos have always been renowned for their theming, Las Vegas used to stick for the most part to desert and Wild West motifs, as with the Frontier and the Sahara. The last twenty years, however, have witnessed the construction of an amazing succession of replica cities. "San Francisco" and "London" are said to be next, and it can only be a matter of time before "Las Vegas" itself appears.

▲ Eiffel Tower

A clear improvement on the original, as it straddles the entire city of Paris and offers views all the way to Italy – sort of.

P.73 ▸ THE CENTRAL STRIP

▲ The Grand Canal

The gondolas in Venice, Italy, tend to stick to sea level; here they're floating around upstairs as well, opera-singing gondoliers and all.

P.83 ▸ THE CENTRAL STRIP

▶ Luxor Pyramid

Is it too late to mention that there aren't in fact any pyramids in Luxor, Egypt? But then, it's the rare pyramid with a casino inside.

P.54 ▶ THE SOUTH STRIP

▲ Monte Carlo

It makes perfect sense for one of Las Vegas's more refined and sedate casinos to evoke the look and feel of the Old World's best-known gambling city.

P.61 ▶ THE SOUTH STRIP

▼ New York–New York

The most fully realized of all the themed casinos slaps the Big Apple down in the heart of the Big Cheese.

P.57 ▶ THE SOUTH STRIP

▼ The Colosseum

Surrounded by classical statuary and fountains, the Colosseum makes a great centerpiece for Caesars' loving (if somewhat addled) reconstruction of ancient Rome.

P.77 ▶ THE CENTRAL STRIP

Kids' Las Vegas

Even though Las Vegas no longer claims to rival Orlando as a kid-friendly destination, it still offers plenty for children to see and enjoy. The over-the-top architecture of the Strip appeals to the child in everyone, but there are also lots of specific attractions to help while away an hour or two when the pool has begun to pall. Older children will also like the thrill rides on p.34.

▲ The Adventuredome

A fully-fledged theme park, with plenty for younger kids, too, under a dome at the back of the generally child-friendly Circus Circus hotel.

P.105 ▶ THE NORTH STRIP

▲ Shark Reef

A surprisingly well-stocked aquarium at Mandalay Bay, abounding in the most colorful and/or ferocious species on the planet.

P.53 ▶ THE SOUTH STRIP

▼ Madame Tussaud's

Pose, preen, and play with all your favorite stars at this Venetian outpost of the international waxworks chain.

P.84 ▶ THE CENTRAL STRIP

▲ Excalibur

Of course this fantasy fairy-tale castle conceals a casino, but it also holds countless treasures for kids, including a large play arcade downstairs.

P.55 ▶ THE SOUTH STRIP

▼ Secret Garden and Dolphin Habitat

Siegfried and Roy don't perform anymore at the Mirage, but you can still see their famed white lions and tigers, and also watch dolphins perform.

P.81 ▶ THE CENTRAL STRIP

▲ GameWorks

This state-of-the-art video arcade has all the latest games, plus a climbing wall and other attractions. There's also pool tables and a bar for any chaperoning adults.

P.60 ▶ THE SOUTH STRIP

Free Las Vegas

Most things that look free in Las Vegas really aren't. You can certainly get free drinks (and occasionally a free room) in casinos, but only as long as you keep gambling. However, you can also see and do a whole lot in the city without spending a cent – in fact many of the free attractions laid on by casinos to lure in passers-by are more exciting than the expensive options inside.

▲ The Fountains

Spectacular sound-and-light water ballets play upon Bellagio's replica of Italy's Lake Como every evening – the perfect place to see water fountains "dance" to classical favorites.

P.75 ▸ THE CENTRAL STRIP

▲ The Fremont Street Experience

And it really is an experience; where else on earth would they roof over an entire street downtown to play videos of multicolored snakes and aliens on the ceiling?

P.112 ▸ DOWNTOWN

▲ The Strip at night

Ablaze at night with neon and giant LED screens (and crowded by gawking pedestrians), Las Vegas's famous Strip is a true wonder of the world.

P.71 ▸ THE CENTRAL STRIP

▼ The Volcano

Back in 1989, Mirage owner Steve Wynn built this volcano, to entice pedestrians off the Strip and into his casino at night; and they're still lining up to admire its regular blasts.

P.80 ▸ THE CENTRAL STRIP

▲ Sirens of TI

Treasure Island's pirates have long gone, replaced on the Strip-front "moat" by these singing, writhing, scantily-clad lovelies.

P.82 ▸ THE CENTRAL STRIP

▼ The Midway

The heart of Circus Circus is a throwback to the old days, with circus acts performing in the central arena, surrounded by old-fashioned carnival sideshows.

P.105 ▸ THE NORTH STRIP

Thrill rides

Forever eager to attract thrill-seeking visitors, and always quick to embrace the latest technology, Las Vegas casinos make a natural home for roller coasters and high-tech virtual-reality rides. Nobody wants to keep gamblers away from the tables for too long, so the rides tend to be short and sharp, but they're undeniably exciting.

▲ X Scream

Seated on a lurching bench at the top of the Stratosphere a thousand feet above the Strip, the fear here is definitely real rather than virtual.

P.108 ▶ THE NORTH STRIP

▲ Manhattan Express

In New York–New York's popular ride, tiny yellow Manhattan taxi cabs speed out into the open air and loop the loop above the Strip.

P.59 ▶ THE SOUTH STRIP

▲ Speed Ride

Short, sweet, and heart-pumping, a quick-fire roller-coaster race out onto the Strip and back into the Sahara.

P.106 ▸ THE NORTH STRIP

▼ In Search of the Obelisk

A sequence of virtual-reality rides through ancient Egypt: your chance to play Indiana Jones at the Luxor.

P.54 ▸ THE SOUTH STRIP

◄ Star Trek Experience

Though you're satisfyingly shaken and jolted to within an inch of your life, the real fun here is taking part in an actual *Star Trek* adventure.

P.133 ▸ EAST OF THE STRIP

▼ Canyon Blaster

Circus Circus's corkscrew ride is hands down the city's best roller coaster.

P.104 ▸ THE NORTH STRIP

Gambling

Though analysts insists that gambling (or "gaming," as it prefers to be known) is on the decline in Las Vegas, that's only relative. Ninety percent of visitors to the city gamble an average of $500 each; it's just that these days they also spend more on other things. Gambling remains the backdrop to everything that goes on, and the siren call of the slot machines provides a constant soundtrack in the casinos.

▲ Craps

For fast and furious action, this quick-fire dice game is unbeatable – though utterly inscrutable to novices.

P.176 › ESSENTIALS

▲ Roulette

The definitive casino game, where every spin of the wheel promises an instant fortune.

P.177 › ESSENTIALS

▲ Race and Sports Books

Whenever and wherever there's a big sports event going on, the atmosphere in these high-tech betting parlors is positively electric.

P.178 ▸ ESSENTIALS

▲ Blackjack

The one card game that everyone still seems to know is a special favorite of gamblers with the brainpower to play by the "system."

P.175 ▸ ESSENTIALS

▼ Poker

The city hasn't completely changed: hustlers and hicks still congregate in Vegas casinos for mammoth poker sessions, especially downtown.

P.176 ▸ ESSENTIALS

▲ Slots

"Real" gamblers may scoff at slot machines, but simply drop a coin in as you check out, and an instant jackpot just might pay for your whole vacation.

P.177 ▸ ESSENTIALS

Classic Las Vegas

Las Vegas is hardly sentimental about its past. As soon as the revenue or foot traffic at any casino or attraction starts to dwindle, it's liable to be torn down and replaced with something bigger and better. Here and there, though – especially downtown – you'll come across reminders of Las Vegas as it used to be, in the old days when the stars shone larger than life and the Mob lurked around every corner.

▲ Liberace Museum

Your chance to get a glimpse inside the great man's boudoir – as fascinating as it is mind-blowingly kitschy.

P.135 ▸ EAST OF THE STRIP

▼ The Flamingo

Bugsy Siegel's original Strip casino is still going strong, with plenty of pink-tinged flair.

P.178 ▸ THE CENTRAL STRIP

▲ A Little White Chapel

It's always a great day for a white wedding in Las Vegas at this venerable chapel.

P.111 ▸ THE NORTH STRIP

▲ Sam's Town

Though it's not actually particularly old, the Sam's Town casino, far removed from the Strip, offers a taste of Las Vegas gambling as it was before the moguls moved in.

P.136 ▸ EAST OF THE STRIP

▶ Binion's Horseshoe

The most atmospheric of the downtown casinos, laid low by scandals and mismanagement, but still a haven for serious gamblers.

P.115
▸ DOWNTOWN

Museums and galleries

For a brief period around the turn of the millennium, it looked as though Las Vegas might actually go highbrow. Steve Wynn was displaying his art collection at the Bellagio, and the Venetian boasted two separate Guggenheim museums. Since Wynn sold out, and the larger of the Guggenheims closed, that moment seems to have passed. Even so, the city still holds some stimulating museums and galleries.

▲ Las Vegas Natural History Museum

Stuffed and live animals, and some overpowering animatronic dinosaurs; one of the few non-casino attractions in Las Vegas that's worth visiting.

P.119 ▸ DOWNTOWN

▲ Guggenheim Hermitage

Small but very choice exhibitions of paintings from St Petersburg's Hermitage museum, displayed in exquisite surroundings at the Venetian.

P.83 ▸ THE CENTRAL STRIP

▲ Auto Collection

These days it's as much of a retail show-room as a museum, but the classic cars and bikes exhibited at Imperial Palace are still a must-see for auto fans.

`P.79 ▸ THE CENTRAL STRIP`

▼ Bellagio Gallery of Fine Art

Though it's been ailing since Wynn's departure, the temporary exhibitions in this small space can still be very rewarding.

`P.76 ▸ THE CENTRAL STRIP`

Viva Las Vegas

The link between Elvis Presley and Las Vegas stretches back some fifty years, from his first concert here in 1956 to his triumphant 1969 return to live performance at the Hilton. Though it's been decades since he finally left the building, the King is very much alive and well in his spiritual home, with singing, sweating lookalikes still putting the Viva into Las Vegas almost everywhere you look.

▲ Legends In Concert

Elvis brings matters to a rousing nightly climax in Las Vegas's best impersonator show, at Imperial Palace.

P.94 ▸ THE CENTRAL STRIP

▲ Elvis-A-Rama

The finest collection of Elvis memorabilia outside of Graceland; just don't step on his blue suede shoes.

P.105 ▸ THE NORTH STRIP

▲ Graceland Wedding Chapel

For that perfect Las Vegas wedding, let the
King serenade you as you walk down the aisle.

P.122 ▶ DOWNTOWN

▶ The Hilton

Elvis resurrected his career by selling out
837 consecutive shows at the Hilton (originally called the International) between 1969
and 1977; he's now commemorated by a
bronze statue in the lobby.

P.132 ▶ EAST OF THE STRIP

▼ The Sahara

The Sahara served as home to Elvis during
the shooting of *Viva Las Vegas*, and the
racing theme remains stronger than ever,
updated for the NASCAR era.

P.101 ▶ THE NORTH STRIP

The Desert

If you spend all your time on the Strip, you could almost forget that Las Vegas is an aberrant oasis amid some of the most desolately beautiful desert on earth. Fortunately, there are several destinations within easy reach where it's possible to sample the splendor of the local landscape. Further afield is the Grand Canyon, a worthwhile destination even though it's almost three hundred miles away by road.

▲ Red Rock Canyon

Las Vegas's great escape; hike and bike amid stunning red-rock sandscapes just twenty miles from the Strip.

P.144 ▶ DAY TRIPS

▲ Valley of Fire State Park

Lurid desert scenery, bizarre rock formations, and wonderfully remote hiking.

P.150 ▸ DAY TRIPS

▲ Grand Canyon West Rim

Grand Canyon National Park is too far away to see cheaply or easily, but the so-called West Rim makes a more than acceptable alternative.

P.152 ▸ DAY TRIPS

▼ Lake Mead

The deep blue waters of Lake Mead are an astonishing sight in the bleak desert – and all but irresistible to watersports enthusiasts.

P.147 ▸ DAY TRIPS

▲ Hoover Dam

This awesome man-made interruption to the course of the majestic Colorado made it possible for Las Vegas to survive in this inhospitable desert.

P.148 ▸ DAY TRIPS

Las Vegas views

Whether you fly into McCarran Airport or drive up on the interstate, getting your first full view of the Strip is one of the great iconic moments of world travel. Once you're actually staying there, though, it can be hard to hang on to the sense of where you are. For a reminder of the sheer scale of Vegas, head to one of the many great vantage points around the city.

▲ The Stratosphere

Las Vegas's highest point, ideally poised between downtown and the Strip – and even equipped with three ludicrous thrill rides if the vistas below aren't enough.

P.106 ▸ THE NORTH STRIP

▼ VooDoo Lounge

The Rio's rooftop bar makes a great spot for evening views of the lights of the city, with drink in hand.

P.130 ▸ WEST OF THE STRIP

▲ Mount Charleston

Admiring the ancient expanse from high on the flanks of Mount Charleston, you can almost forget modern Las Vegas even exists.

P.146 ▸ DAY TRIPS

◀ Helicopter ride

There's no better way to see the Strip at night than swooping above it in a chopper.

P.171 ▸ ESSENTIALS

▼ The Eiffel Tower

Ride the escalators of this Parisian replica to command superb views of the very heart of the Strip.

P.73 ▸ THE CENTRAL STRIP

Places

The South Strip

Broadly speaking, the Strip has been creeping steadily southward for the last sixty years, the empty spaces tempting developers with the twin advantages of room to build and proximity to the airport. When Excalibur opened just south of Tropicana Boulevard in 1990, it was seen as a daring move, but since then both Luxor and Mandalay Bay have pushed further south still, and more will no doubt follow. Mandalay Bay's high-quality nightlife and dining in particular lure hordes of visitors down the Strip, and with New York–New York and the MGM Grand also thriving at the Tropicana intersection, the Strip's southern segment has become every bit as important as its older central section.

Mandalay Bay

3950 Las Vegas Blvd S ☎877/632-7800, ⓦwww.mandalaybay.com. Glowing like beacons as their gilded windows commandeer the sunset, the twin forty-story sentinels of Mandalay Bay mark the southern limits of the Strip. The casino's opening in 1999 represented the next step in the upwards progress of Circus Circus Enterprises, each of whose previous properties (from Circus Circus itself, to Excalibur, and then Luxor) had been significantly more upmarket. With Mandalay Bay, the company aimed itself squarely at a younger and more affluent generation of customers, and even renamed itself the Mandalay Resort Group. The casino has been so successful that a second thousand-room tower, *THEhotel*, was added in 2004, while the company itself was bought out by the competitors it originally aimed to match, and now belongs to MGM-Mirage.

Although the name "Mandalay Bay" is supposed to conjure up romantic images from Rudyard Kipling's poem *The*

▲ HOUSE OF BLUES, MANDALAY BAY

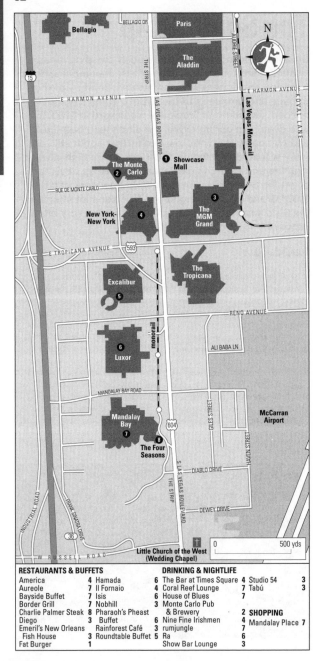

RESTAURANTS & BUFFETS

America	4	Hamada	6
Aureole	7	Il Fornaio	7
Bayside Buffet	7	Isis	7
Border Grill	7	Nobhill	7
Charlie Palmer Steak	8	Pharaoh's Pheast	
Diego	3	Buffet	6
Emeril's New Orleans		Rainforest Café	3
Fish House		Roundtable Buffet	5
Fat Burger	1		

DRINKING & NIGHTLIFE

The Bar at Times Square	4	Studio 54	3
Coral Reef Lounge	7	Tabú	3
House of Blues	7		
Monte Carlo Pub			
& Brewery	3		
Nine Fine Irishmen	4		
rumjungle	7		
Ra	6		
Show Bar Lounge	3		

SHOPPING

Mandalay Place	7

STATUE OF LENIN, MANDALAY BAY

Road to Mandalay, the theming here is very generic. Landscaped gardens and walkways abound in Asiatic motifs, but otherwise Mandalay Bay makes little effort to entertain rubbernecking tourists. Instead it combines an overall soft-focus tropical feel with a full-on resort experience for its guests, who get to enjoy a superb open-air pool complex, featuring a sandy beach and the "Lazy River" tubing ride.

When the Hacienda was built on this site back in 1955 – it was finally blown up on New Year's Eve, 1996 – it stood well over a mile south of the Strip. Although an unbroken chain of casinos now stretches all the way here, Mandalay Bay is still perceived as off the beaten track. Few pedestrians brave the long, discouraging slog to get here; hence the rudimentary feel of the Strip-level entrance. Most casual visitors instead get their first impression of the property arriving on the free monorail from Excalibur and Luxor, or walking through the covered **Mandalay Place** mall, lined with specialty stores and res-

taurants, that connects Luxor and Mandalay Bay.

It's at night that Mandalay Bay really comes alive. Boasting over a dozen top-class eateries along its "**Restaurant Row**" certainly helps, but the cornerstone of the casino's strategy to lure hip customers is the **House of Blues** music venue. For really major events, like boxing matches, Mandalay Bay also has its own 12,000-seat arena, while the Abba musical *Mamma Mia!* plays in a separate theater. The crowds that spill out when the show's over tend to stick around into the small hours, grazing in the late-night lounges or gambling in the massive, ultra-modern Race and Sports Book.

Mandalay Bay's one major attraction for sightseers, the popular **Shark Reef** aquarium (daily 10am–11pm; $16, under-12s $10, or $38/$34 combined with the Luxor attractions; ☎702/632-4555), is a long walk from the Strip-facing front of the property, far beyond the end of Restaurant Row. The emphasis in "North America's only predator-based aquarium" is more on eye-catching monsters than education, with video displays rather than written captions next to each tank. The basic premise is that you're exploring a steamy, half-submerged temple complex, encountering crocodiles, jellyfish, and (of course) sharks. Sharing these creatures' living quarters are some miserable-looking fish, many bearing large bite marks and missing portions of their anatomy. An excitable marine biologist provides a running commentary on "audio-wands," (no charge) though for all his expertise he's somehow failed to spot that all the so-called "coral" on offer is actually multicolored plastic.

Luxor

3900 Las Vegas Blvd S ☎ 888/777-0188, ⓦ www.luxor.com. When it opened in 1993, Luxor was heralded as the ultimate in-your-face Las Vegas casino. A forbidding 350ft-high pyramid of black glass, it dominated the southern approach to the Strip, its colossal Sphinx seemingly standing guard over not merely this one casino but all the splendors of the city. These days, however, it's surprisingly easy to forget that Luxor is even there, not least because its owners have overshadowed it by building the more glamorous Mandalay Bay next door. The entire exterior is so featureless that it's hard to get much sense of its vast scale, while being constructed out of black glass makes the pyramid even more inconspicuous (especially at night). That said, Luxor has been a great financial success, and ongoing improvements make it likely to be so for some time.

In theory, Luxor is approached from the Strip sidewalk via a palm-fringed avenue of ram-headed sphinxes, but usually the only pedestrians out there are hotel guests briefly braving the sun for a photo opportunity. The monorail that connects Luxor with Excalibur and Mandalay Bay drops its passengers in front of the Sphinx, which doubles as a *porte-cochère*, its vast belly sheltering the vehicles that drive between its paws.

The spectacle inside is every bit as dramatic. The interior of the hollow pyramid is a vast open space ringed by concentric levels of guest rooms, the world's largest atrium at 29 million cubic feet (though unfortunately none of the elevators climbing up the inner walls offer any views down). To reach the casino, you pass through a reconstruction of Abu Simbel temple, guarded by two huge, seated statues. The gaming area itself is no more exciting than any other, but it's surrounded by friezes, statues, hieroglyphic inscriptions, and other Pharaonic paraphernalia. Luxor employees in gold costumes patrol the precincts, posing for photos.

Luxor's 36 stories taper to a point overhead, with the most powerful artificial **light beam** ever created shining up from the very apex. Though said to be visible from outer space, from the ground it's barely noticeable amid the general neon glare of the Strip. Around the back of the pyramid, the large swimming pool – open to guests only, and very short on shade – is overlooked by more counterfeit

▼ TOMB OF KING TUTANKHAMUN

▲ SPHINX OUTSIDE LUXOR

IMAX ride films ($6.50–7.50), not always Egyptian-themed, which subject viewers to nauseating mechanical bumps and lurches.

Excalibur

3850 Las Vegas Blvd S ☎877/750-5464, ⓦwww.excalibur.com. The oldest of the three adjacent casinos constructed by the Mandalay Resort Group (formerly Circus Circus), the mocked-up medieval castle of Excalibur now makes a crude and unsophisticated neighbor for Luxor and Mandalay Bay. Hastily erected in 1990, in the hope of outdoing the then-new Mirage, it only cost half as much to build, and it shows, appearing to be both designed and assembled by children, with its oversized primary-colored turrets drawn straight from a kindergarten art class.

In building Excalibur, architect Veldon Simpson – later also responsible for both the MGM Grand and Luxor – took as his inspiration the castle of Neuschwanstein, built in Bavaria in the nineteenth century by Mad King Ludwig, who stuck the fairy-tale flourishes of a French château atop the redoubtable walls of a German fortress. Excalibur's colors are deliberately clashing, and its proportions distorted. It's basically a gigantic billboard, the castle all but engulfed by the two huge hotel towers that hold its four thousand guest rooms. For its first three years, Excalibur was the world's largest hotel, and profitable enough to finance the building of Luxor next door. At the root of that success was its appeal to families and low-budget tour groups. Even now that it's aging, Excalibur's popularity with family vacationers remains undimmed.

colossi, as well as several thousand more hotel rooms and a couple of huge parking lots.

The **Attractions Level** in Luxor (Mon–Thurs & Sun 9am–11pm, Fri & Sat 9am–1am, hours vary seasonally; attractions priced individually, $25 "Passport to Adventure" covers all, combined ticket with Mandalay Bay's Shark Reef $38, under-12s $34), reached via escalators from the casino floor, is the one place where the property's theming goes wrong. Supposedly this area represents "the future," but its half-hearted "skyscrapers" are more a weird hybrid of modern New York and medieval Cairo. Amid the uninspired mess are a small food court, a couple of restaurants, and a games arcade. A meticulous replica of the **Tomb of King Tutankhamun** ($5) attempts to strike a highbrow note, though most visitors who shuffle through appear bemused by its ersatz treasures. After all, the original – which stands across the River Nile from Luxor, Egypt – remained undiscovered for millennia precisely because it was so small and pokey. Nearby, an auditorium offers a changing program of

▲ MERLIN WATCHES OVER EXCALIBUR

The pedestrian entrance to Excalibur from the Strip incorporates the monorail station for Mandalay Bay. The castle itself is then approached via lengthy moving walkways, on which almost no expense has been lavished. A purple-robed figure of Merlin waves benignly from the central turret, while a booming, genial English voice welcomes all "loyal subjects" to King Arthur's domain of Camelot.

Once inside, you're plunged as ever into the maelstrom of the casino floor, unique for the Strip in allowing visitors to take photographs of the gambling action. For once, however, it's easy to escape to the non-gaming areas. Upstairs you'll find most of Excalibur's uninspiring assortment of restaurants, together with a bunch of "shoppes," a food court, and assorted family-fun opportunities. Downstairs from the casino, on the other hand, the atmosphere is reminiscent of a traditional fairground, along the lines of Circus Circus' Midway, filled with sideshows where kids can spend real money attempting to win plastic swords and other Arthurian memorabilia.

The Tropicana

3801 Las Vegas Blvd S ☏ 888/826-8767, ⓦ www.tropicanalv.com. On its opening day in 1957, the Tropicana stood a mile removed from the body of the Strip, and considered itself as a class apart. Reportedly bankrolled by the New Orleans Mafia, the so-called "Tiffany of the Strip" – the nickname owes to the stained-glass ceiling that hangs above its central gaming tables – was aimed squarely at high-rollers, and its flamboyant paradise-island trimmings epitomized Las Vegas luxury. These days, however, the Tropicana palls in comparison to its mighty neighbors, and is widely expected to close for redevelopment soon. For the moment, its continued profitability depends on refugees from Excalibur and the MGM Grand who cross the pedestrian bridges over the Strip and Tropicana Avenue either to find a more traditional place to gamble, or simply to escape the kids.

Though the "tropical" theme of the "Island of Las Vegas" is pretty vague, and not based on any specific location, that didn't stop the Tropicana from trying to sue the Mirage for allegedly copying the idea in 1989. Appropriately enough, its facade now suspiciously resembles the Caribbean village at the Mirage's sister property, TI, minus the Sirens but plus false storefronts in pastel colors. The corresponding shops can be found within, just not behind the relevant "doors."

Near the Tropicana's main entrance, all visitors are invited to take a free pull on a giant slot machine; everyone wins at least discount coupons or show tickets. The interior is a muddled maze offering scant reward to

How the Strip began

Little more than fifty years ago, as Hwy-51, Las Vegas Boulevard was just a dusty desert thoroughfare, scattered with the occasional edge-of-town motel as it set off south toward California. Now, as a four-mile showcase of the most extravagant architecture on earth, it's a tourist destination in its own right, the most popular in the US, except for Orlando.

The boulevard was nicknamed "The Strip" because it reminded former LA police captain Guy McAfee of the Sunset Strip. McAfee moved to Las Vegas in 1938, after being obliged to resign because he controlled a string of illegal gambling joints, and took over the boulevard's first casino, the Pair-O-Dice Club. Over the next ten years, it was joined on the Strip by El Rancho, in 1941, the Last Frontier in 1942, Bugsy Siegel's legendary Flamingo in 1946, and the Thunderbird in 1948.

For casino owners, much of the appeal of the nascent Strip was that it lay outside city limits in Clark County, where they could dominate what little political life there was, sparing themselves the scrutiny suffered by their rivals downtown. Their control of the county machine enabled them to resist repeated attempts to bring the Strip under the jurisdiction of the city authorities, and they've been free to pursue untrammeled development ever since.

those who try to penetrate it. Until 2005, it was home to the Casino Legends Hall of Fame, an entertaining museum of gambling history, but that's currently looking for a new location (@www.nevadamint .com). The gallery where it was housed now plays host instead to large-scale temporary exhibitions.

Where the Tropicana really does come up trumps is with its **swimming pool**, which is among the best in Las Vegas. Covering five landscaped acres, it's more of a waterpark really,

surrounded by lush gardens and complete with hot tubs, fish-filled lagoons, a swim-up bar, and an outdoor wedding chapel.

New York–New York

3790 Las Vegas Blvd S ☎888/696-9887, @www.nynyhotelcasino .com. The craze for creating counterfeit cities in Las Vegas was spearheaded by the 1997 construction of New York–New York, an entire metropolis compressed into a single structure. The motives behind the creation of this miniature

▼ POOL AT THE TROPICANA

Manhattan were much the same as for the real one; when space is at a premium, the best way to build is upward. Thanks to an exuberant attention to detail, it's a triumph.

From street level, New York–New York looks stunning, its twelve pastel skyscrapers silhouetted sharply against the blue desert sky. Apart from the proud **Statue of Liberty** (just over twice the size of the original) at the front, the mock skyline's various components are between a third and a half as big as their East Coast counterparts. Perhaps mercifully, the copycat towers never included the World Trade Center; instead, the highest point is the 510-foot, 47-story **Empire State Building**. This squashed-up cityscape is not simply a static tableau. Matching red and green fireboats jet arcs of water across a tiny New York Harbor, while above, a Coney Island–style roller coaster loops and swoops around the skyline in full view – and earshot – of the Strip.

For once, New York–New York is as much fun inside as out. Not that the distinction is all that clear; there's only a minimal correlation between the interior and the exterior, so you step through the doors

made up to look like Grand Central Station to find yourself not safely inside the terminal, but walking through Central Park at nightfall. Stuffed owls gaze down on the gaming tables from fake trees strung with fairy lights, and the carpeted walkways are disguised as footpaths strewn with fallen leaves. The one drawback to this design is that the narrow aisles often feel overcrowded with sightseers – not unlike the real city.

As well as the obligatory casino and its elegant "Guys" and "Dolls" restrooms, the ground floor holds several unexpected delights. The **Greenwich Village** section comes complete not only with delis, fast-food outlets, and a fake subway station, but even fire hydrants, trashcans, and mailboxes, all sprayed with impressive (if firmly PG-rated) graffiti. Elevators up to the hotel rooms leave from lobbies styled to resemble specific buildings – one reproduces the Art Deco embellishments of the Chrysler Building.

Most of the upper floor of New York–New York is given over to the **Coney Island Emporium** (daily 8.30am–2am; attractions individually priced), a truly staggering array of

▼ NEW YORK–NEW YORK

▲ CASINO AT NEW YORK–NEW YORK

carnival sideshows, video games, and other kids' attractions. New York theming is everywhere you look, including some great bumper cars dolled up as yellow taxis.

To reach New York–New York's most popular and eye-catching attraction, the **Manhattan Express roller coaster** (Mon–Thurs 11am–11pm, Fri & Sat 10am–midnight, Sun 10am–11pm; $12.50 first ride, $6 subsequent rides, $25 all-day Scream Pass), you have first to shuffle for a considerable period along the walkways of a mocked-up subway station that adjoins Coney Island. After boarding the roller coaster's little yellow taxicabs you hurtle very briefly above the casino floor, then race out into the open air on a juddering ride that reaches speeds of 65mph, and spirals through some fearsomely tight rolls. Not an experience theme-park neophytes should undertake lightly, this is one of Las Vegas's very best thrill rides, matched only by the roller coaster at Circus Circus's Adventuredome.

MGM Grand

3799 Las Vegas Blvd S ☎877/880-0880, ⓦwww.mgmgrand.com. A lot of careful planning went into the construction of what remains, at least until the Venetian's planned expansion, Las Vegas's largest hotel, the MGM Grand – most of it turned out to be hopelessly wrong. In the early 90s, when Las Vegas saw itself as the family destination of the future, this billion-dollar project staked its prospects on a theme park. From the moment it opened in 1993, however, the theme park was panned, and it has long since closed down. Indeed, the whole idea of luring children into casinos seems to have had its day. And yet the MGM Grand itself somehow never floundered, going from strength to strength.

Spreading over 114 acres, the Grand is bigger than Luxor and Excalibur combined. Its owner, Armenian billionaire Kirk Kerkorian – like Howard Hughes, a former aviator – has twice before erected the world's largest hotel. The first is what's now the Las Vegas Hilton; the second, also originally called the MGM Grand, became Bally's after the horrific 1980 fire (see p.74). One way in which the Grand copes with its sheer size is by not having one obvious main entrance, thus dispersing

▲ LION STATUE, MGM GRAND

the crowds. Pedestrians arrive straight off the Strip at ground level, or via first-floor walkways from New York–New York and the Tropicana, to either side of a seventy-foot bronze lion. Hotel guests and all other traffic use a separate entrance a hundred yards east along Tropicana Avenue, while Monorail passengers disembark at the back of the property, a very long walk from the hotel lobby.

The one real concession to casual sightseers at the MGM Grand is the **Lion Habitat**, beside the casino floor not far off the Strip (daily 11am–11pm; free).

Shamelessly taking a leaf from the Mirage and its tigers, this glass enclosure holds real lions that lounge around a faux ruined temple beneath a naturally lit dome. Visitors can stroll through a glass tunnel as lions pad directly overhead or they can participate in the grotesque charade of having a photo taken (daily except Tues 11am–5pm; $20) with a cute little cub that's made to look wistful and winsome by having its milk bottle whisked away for a fraction of a second.

There is, however, plenty at the Grand to satisfy anyone looking for something to do, from nightclubs and show lounges

to a mouthwatering array of restaurants and the theaters that host *Kà* and *La Femme*. Given the wealth of attractions on hand, it's hardly surprising that the place is always crowded – and it becomes even more so whenever a big-name boxing match or rock concert is staged in its fifteen-thousand-seat arena. As for the MGM Grand's vast **casino**, just to stock the slot machines in the first place required thirteen million quarters (that's $3.25 million). Turnover on its gaming tables is so phenomenal that when the crowds hanging around after the Holyfield–Tyson ear-biting debacle mistook the popping of champagne corks for gunfire, and the resulting furor forced the casino to close down for two hours, the casino's loss was estimated in millions of dollars.

Showcase Mall

3769 Las Vegas Blvd S ☎702/597-3122. Immediately north of the MGM Grand, the Showcase Mall is a rarity for the Strip – a shiny modern development that's not a casino. The general trend away from catering to kids, however, coupled with the lack of gambling revenue, probably explains why it's floundered in recent years, with both the World of Coca-Cola "museum" and the *All-Star Cafe* forced to close their doors. An eight-screen movie theater here (the only one on the Strip) does good business, but the main attraction is **GameWorks** (Mon–Thurs & Sun 10am–midnight, Fri & Sat 10am–2am; unlimited play starting at $20/hr; ☎702/432-4263, ⓦwww.gameworks.com), a Spielberg-owned arcade of

▲ GAMEWORKS

▲ THE MONTE CARLO

video and virtual-reality games, as well as a 75-foot rock-climbing wall. The rest of the mall holds a jumble of rather nondescript souvenir stores and fast-food outlets.

The Monte Carlo

3770 Las Vegas Blvd S ☎888/529-4828, ⓦ www.monte-carlo.com. The Monte Carlo, which opened in 1996, has to be the soberest new casino to appear in Las Vegas since the early 90s. Built as a joint venture between the Mandalay Resort Group and MGM-Mirage, long before their recent merger, its serene appearance signaled a reluctance to impinge on its more flamboyant neighbors. True, its exterior, nominally modeled on the Place du Casino in Monte Carlo, is forever acquiring more Rococo flourishes and sub-Caesars statuary, and there's a certain Belle Epoque elegance about its plush trimmings. However, apart from its ornate 1200-seat **Lance Burton Theater**, the theming does not extend to its restaurants and other facilities, and is of minimal significance to most guests. They tend to be

an affluent and slightly older-than-average group, who see the Monte Carlo as being a quieter and classier place to both sleep and gamble than almost anywhere on the Strip. The one place the guests can let their hair down is the *Monte Carlo Pub & Brewery*, at the far end of an unassuming shopping mall known fancifully as the Street of Dreams.

Restaurants

America

New York–New York, 3790 Las Vegas Blvd S ☎702/740-6451. Daily 24hr.
A cavernous diner, tucked in behind the registration desk, which derives its retro-chic feel from a vast 3-D "map" of the US (measuring 30x90ft) that curls down from the ceiling. Each menu item supposedly comes from some specific part of the country. Thus appetizers include Wild West potato skins from Boise ($7) and lobster chop stix from Seattle ($9), while entrees range from Texan barbecue ribs ($14), via New York pizzas ($9–11), down to a tuna melt from Reno ($8.50). At any hour of the day or night, there really is something here for everyone, and it's all surprisingly good.

Aureole

Mandalay Bay, 3950 Las Vegas Blvd S ☎702/632-7401, ⓦ www.ewinetower.com. Dinner only.
Welcome to wine-lover's heaven, where harnessed "wine angels" swoop around a three-story "wine tower" that holds 10,000 bottles. Diners use tablet PCs to peruse the online wine list, with prices ranging from $36,000 (for a 1900 Château Petrus Pomerol) down to $21 for an unassuming

Lebanese white. New York chef Charlie Palmer's "Progressive American Cuisine" is every bit as impressive, making *Aureole* a strong contender for Las Vegas's best restaurant. Choose between a prix-fixe menu on which $85 buys a substantial appetizer and entree, or the changing $95 "Celebration Menu," which features up to eight smaller courses, plus the odd *amuse-bouche* and "pre-dessert." Standout dishes, all beautifully presented, include the curry-nut-crusted tuna, the halibut topped with a black-truffle foam, and the pork chop stuffed with prosciutto and gruyère.

Border Grill

Mandalay Bay, 3950 Las Vegas Blvd S ☎702/632-7403. This classy Mexican restaurant at the back of Mandalay Bay, run by TV chefs Mary Sue Milliken and Susan Feniger, comes into its own during summer, when tables spread out across an open-air patio towards the spectacular wave pool, but even in winter its high ceilings and light decor give it a spacious feel. Steer clear of the very ordinary *ceviche* for lunch, and focus instead on the tacos ($9–12) and entrees ($14 and up). Dinner is more expensive, with slow-roasted pork in black *mole* sauce at $19 and a 12oz gaucho steak for $28.

Charlie Palmer Steak

Four Seasons, 3960 Las Vegas Blvd S ☎702/632-5210, ⓦwww .charliepalmersteaklv.com. Dinner only. Tucked away from the hubbub of Mandalay Bay amid the ultra-quiet marble corridors of the *Four Seasons* (see p.160), the sophisticated, dimly lit *Charlie Palmer Steak* feels more like a New York gentlemen's club than a new Las Vegas nightspot. The menu is also less showy than at Palmer's contrasting *Aureole*; in fact, you could opt for an utterly traditional $15 prawn cocktail followed by a 22oz rib-eye steak for $40 and imagine the last forty years never happened. The beef, all aged 28 days, is invariably superb, and the main reason why people come, but there's also a delicious pan-seared halibut for $29, as well as plenty of chicken, lamb, and so on, not to mention an amazing *foie gras* "BLT" appetizer.

Diego

MGM Grand, 3799 Las Vegas Blvd S ☎702/891-1111. Both menu and decor at MGM's excellent Mexican restaurant, near the Monorail station at the back of the property, blend Mexican tradition with contemporary design (check out the restrooms for an especially striking combination). The painstakingly prepared food is modeled on home cooking from southern Mexico. At both lunch and dinner appetizers like guacamole, crab empanadas, and the shrimp and lobster

▼ EMERIL'S NEW ORLEANS FISH HOUSE

ceviche cost $7–12, while entrees include *arroz a la tumbada*, a sort of Mexican paella, for $19 at lunch, $27 dinner; chicken in a delicate red *mole* sauce ($17/$24); and slow-cooked marinated pork ($18/$24). For dinner, they also offer a $6 mixed plate of organic vegetables, while the $6 desserts range from ice-cream sandwiches to Mexican crêpes. You can even get a $4 margarita popsicle.

▲ IL FORNAIO

Emeril's New Orleans Fish House

MGM Grand, 3799 Las Vegas Blvd S ☎702/891-7374. Renowned TV chef Emeril Lagasse has revamped his original Las Vegas outpost to give it a more stylish and contemporary feel, but the food itself remains as drenched in New Orleans flavor as ever. While Cajun seafood with a modern (but never low-cal) twist is the specialty – there's barbecue shrimp as a $12 appetizer and redfish in *creole meunière* sauce as a $25 entree – the menu also includes meat options like herb-roasted chicken ($28) and cedar-plank steak ($35). Yes, the waiters do say "Bam" as they deliver each dish. If you find the entrees gut-bustingly rich, wait until you see the desserts; but it's all so fabulous you can't help throwing dietary caution to the winds.

Fat Burger

3765 Las Vegas Blvd S ☎702/736-4733. Daily 24hr. There's no more than meets the eye to this gleaming, all-American burger joint just north of Showcase Mall, and that's a very good thing. Quite simply, you can walk or drive in from the Strip at any time, and get a perfect, substantial, juicy burger, plus fries and a shake.

Hamada

Luxor, 3900 Las Vegas Blvd S ☎702/262-4549, ⊛www.hamadaofjapan.com. Las Vegas's best sushi chain has several branches, including outlets at the MGM Grand, the Flamingo, and the Stratosphere, as well as this one near Luxor's front entrance. Daily lunch specials cost $9–12, while a full sashimi meal is $25 during the day or $40 in the evening.

Il Fornaio

New York–New York, 3790 Las Vegas Blvd S ☎702/650-6500, ⊛www.ilfornaio.com. The nicest place to enjoy the atmosphere of New York–New York, offering both a high-ceilinged "indoor" dining room (complete with open kitchen) and terrace seating alongside Central Park, this rural-Italian restaurant, staffed by very flirtatious waiters who speak Italian among themselves, is a real joy. Grab a pizza for around $12, or linger over a full meal, perhaps the lovely eggplant salad, with goat cheese and smoked salmon ($9.50) to start, followed by seafood linguini ($19), rotisserie chicken ($16), or a boneless leg of lamb with garlic ($23). *Il Fornaio's* delicious olive breads, pastries, and espresso are also sold in the separate deli alongside the front desk.

Isis

Luxor, 3900 Las Vegas Blvd S ☎702/262-4773. Dinner only. A real only-in-Vegas experience, this very classy gourmet restaurant matches any in the city for cuisine, while simultaneously reveling in its high-camp Egyptian trimmings. Guests have to wear "appropriate" formal attire (ties not compulsory) and make their way past an Indiana Jones–style array of gilded statues and columns to get in. You're also obliged to spend at least $40 per person – not hard when vegetables are $8 per portion. Appetizers such as glazed prawns go for around $16, while typical meat entrees like seared veal scaloppine cost $41, seafood or fowl alternatives a little less.

Nobhill

MGM Grand, 3799 Las Vegas Blvd S ☎702/793-7111. Dinner only. The most refined of MGM's impressive fleet of restaurants occupies a formal earth-toned dining room in a prime location not far off the Strip. San Francisco's Michael Mina puts less emphasis on seafood here than at his namesake Bellagio eatery, but otherwise the menu is similar. To sample the full range, opt for a seven-course tasting menu, either the "San Francisco Classic" at $79, or the $110 premium version, but be warned that the portions are often small. For a more substantial meal, you'll have to go à la carte; the signature lobster pot pie, baked in a gleaming copper pan in the bread oven and containing an entire lobster, costs $69, but alternatives like the chicken tetrazzini, on a bed of sublimely incongruous haute-cuisine truffle macaroni cheese, are more reasonably priced.

Rainforest Cafe

MGM Grand, 3799 Las Vegas Blvd S ☎702/891-8580. This exuberant theme restaurant at MGM's Strip entrance boasts the most fabulously over-the-top decor in town, consisting of a dense jungle filled with huts and waterfalls, giant butterflies and animatronic animals. How all that running water helps preserve scarce resources is anyone's guess, but it's a fun and decently-priced place to bring the kids, and the food is pretty good, too. At breakfast, you can have a fruit plate or eggs Benedict for around $10; later on, there's little for newly converted vegetarian eco-warriors, but you can get a burger for $10, pot roast for $15, or a "primal steak" for $23.

Buffets

Bayside Buffet

Mandalay Bay, 3950 Las Vegas Blvd S ☎702/632-7402. Breakfast $13, lunch $15.50, dinner $23. Mandalay Bay's buffet has a nicer setting than most of its rivals, overlooking the resort's pool and open to the breezes when weather permits. The food choice is not all that amazing, though, with none of the usual "stations" devoted to specific cuisines. If you're happy with one or two good roast meats from the carvery, like turkey or beef, plus a few specialty items such as crab legs or paella, you'll be fine; the pre-cut deli sandwiches at lunchtime make a welcome change from the buffet norm.

Pharaoh's Pheast Buffet

Luxor, 3900 Las Vegas Blvd S ☎702/262-4000. Breakfast $10.75, lunch $11.25, dinner $17. As usual at Luxor, the theming at its lower-floor buffet is first-rate, with mummies lying in the desert sands surrounded by golden treasure, and lots of palm trees and columns to provide an intimate atmosphere. For kids, the decor alone makes it the best in the city; most adults, though, find the food unexceptional for the price. Breakfast is particularly unextraordinary.

▲ CORAL REEF LOUNGE

Roundtable Buffet

Excalibur, 3850 Las Vegas Blvd S ☎702/597-7777. Breakfast $9, lunch $10, dinner $14.50. While certainly not the best buffet in town, with a capacity of 1300 the *Roundtable* is the city's largest and busiest option, and it has improved significantly in recent years. The long lines still shuffle straight to the serving counters, making it hard to check out what's on offer – of course the dreariest stuff is near the front – and you have to be seriously assertive to go back for second helpings. In the end, though, most diners seem to leave happy enough with the generally very conventional American food. Watch out for the breakfast bagels, each of which is perhaps a quarter of the size of the smallest bagel you've ever seen in your life.

Bars and lounges

The Bar at Times Square

New York–New York, 3790 Las Vegas Blvd S ☎702/740-6969. Daily 5am–4am, showtime 8pm–2am. Cover $10 Fri & Sat. This rowdy slice of the Big Apple, set in the heart of Central Park, is dominated nightly by twin dueling pianists, who hammer out showtunes and old hits while the capacity crowd sings along at ear-splitting volume.

Coral Reef Lounge

Mandalay Bay, 3950 Las Vegas Blvd S ☎702/632-7777. Daily 24hr. A tropical ocean paradise dropped in the middle of the casino floor, where you can buy drinks and (expensive) sushi at all hours. There's a huge fish tank behind the bar, and pretty good showbands play here nightly.

Monte Carlo Pub & Brewery

Monte Carlo, 3770 Las Vegas Blvd S ☎702/730-7777. Sun–Thurs 11am–2am, Fri & Sat 11am–4am. This massive microbrewery isn't bad for an early-evening drink – the beers produced in its gleaming copper vats taste pretty good – but from 9pm onwards it turns into a deafening retro dance club, usually showcasing low-grade rock bands.

Nine Fine Irishmen

New York–New York, 3790 Las Vegas Blvd S ☎702/740-6463, ⓦwww .ninefineirishmen.com. Sun–Thurs 11am–2.30am, Fri & Sat 11am–3.30am. Cover $5 Wed & Thurs, $10 Fri & Sat. The affinity between New York and all things Irish finds

▲ MONTE CARLO PUB & BREWERY

expression in this two-story wood-paneled pub, shipped over from Ireland and featuring live Irish musicians, singers, and dancers nightly.

Show Bar Lounge

MGM Grand, 3799 Las Vegas Blvd S ☎702/891-1111. Daily 24hr. The MGM's dome-ceilinged main lounge is too large to be very atmospheric, but its huge stage often features the King himself, performing live.

Clubs and music venues

House of Blues

Mandalay Bay, 3950 Las Vegas Blvd S ☎702/632-7600, ⓦwww.hob.com. Happy to play host to this outpost of the burgeoning national live-music chain, Mandalay Bay leaves the *House of Blues* to chart its own voodoo-tinged, folk-art-decorated course, with definite but not exclusive emphasis in its programming toward blues, R&B, and the like. Typical prices range from around $30 for B-list names up to $85 for stars like Aretha Franklin.

Ra

Luxor, 3900 Las Vegas Blvd S ☎702/992-7970. Wed–Sat 10pm–5am. Cover $10 women, $20 men. Despite the gloriously camp Egyptian motifs, including bare-breasted Nile maidens at both entrances, *Ra* feels like a real city nightclub, booking very big-name DJs to cater to a ferociously hip and glamorous crowd that includes a high proportion of locals. Cage dancers watch over a changing schedule of special nights, usually with playful quasi-erotic tinges.

rumjungle

Mandalay Bay, 3950 Las Vegas Blvd S ☎702/632-7408. Mon & Thurs–Sat 5.30pm–4am, Tues & Wed 5.30pm–2am. Cover (for non-diners only) $20. Incredibly popular hybrid bar-restaurant-nightclub, where after waiting in line you still have to run a gauntlet of go-go dancers and volcanic gas jets just to get in. Leopardskin-clad staff serve well-priced cocktails, plus a vast menu of rums, while it's too loud to do anything more than watch the pole dancers above the bar, or join the Latin-tinged action on the (small-ish) dance floor.

Paying for the flame-grilled Brazilian feast ($20–40), served until 11pm, spares you the cover charge.

Studio 54

MGM Grand, 3799 Las Vegas Blvd S ☎702/891-7254, ⓦwww.studio54lv .com. Tues–Sat 10pm–5am. Cover men $10 Tues–Thurs (MGM guests free), $20 Fri & Sat; no cover for women. A three-story, four-dance-floor re-creation of New York's legendary *Studio 54*, complete with surly doormen. A separate upstairs locals' room ensures that it's not totally dominated by tourists. Tuesday's "EDEN" (Erotically Delicious Entertain-ers' Night) party is the best time to come; otherwise, the music varies little from night to night, rarely straying from house and other forms of electronica.

Tabú

MGM Grand, 3799 Las Vegas Blvd S ☎702/891-7183. Tues–Sun 10pm–5am. Cover $20. The definitive Las Vegas "ultra-lounge;" not only do go-go girls dance on the tables, but the tables themselves respond to touch by dancing with swirling colors. Expert and beautiful staff mix any cocktail, while, despite the lack of a proper dance floor, they host themed nights like "Slide" (old-school hip hop) on Sundays, or the more general "Dolce Vita" on Thursdays.

Shows

Folies Bergere

The Tropicana, 3801 Las Vegas Blvd S ☎702/739-2411. Mon, Wed, Thurs & Sat 7.30pm & 10pm (topless), Tues & Fri 8.30pm (topless); all shows except 7:30pm over-16s only. $45–55. A fixture at the Tropicana since

1959, the *Folies Bergere* is the longest-running show in the US. While there have been changes over the years, the basic formula remains the same: a mildly "naughty" Parisian revue designed to blow the minds of stout, bearded farmers from Iowa. Showgirls with fixed grins and feathered headdresses – and topless at times during certain performances – high-kick and waltz through a succession of big production numbers, with a break while quick-fire Mexican juggler Wally Eastwood plays the piano with his balls. All the music is recorded, with sequences designed to reflect each of the first six decades of the twentieth century rounded off by a rather outdated tribute to the "modern" woman, who, we are solemnly informed, "has not abandoned her sexuality."

Hairspray

Luxor, 3900 Las Vegas Blvd S ☎888/777-0188, ⓦwww.luxor .com. After Luxor lost Blue Man Group to the Venetian in 2005, they renovated their 1500-seat theater and plugged in an abbreviated, 90-minute, intermission-less version of the 2003 Tony-winning musical, *Hairspray*. Although yet to open at the time of writing, the musical (based on John Waters' film about rock'n'roll and inte-gration in 1960s Baltimore)

▲ FOLIES BERGERE

should still be the same puffy, family-friendly show packed with catchy songs and infectious dance numbers that it was on Broadway.

Kà

MGM Grand, 3799 Las Vegas Blvd S ☎702/891-7777, ⓦwww.ka.com. Fri–Tues 7pm & 10:30pm. $99, $125, $150. For anyone interested in theater, Las Vegas's fourth Cirque de Soleil production, *Kà*, is an absolute must-see. With a budget of $165 million, and nightly cast of 75 performers and 158 technicians, it's the most expensive theatrical production ever staged anywhere; in fact it goes way beyond conventional notions of "theater" to seem more like a feature film, in particular martial arts spectaculars like *Crouching Tiger, Hidden Dragon*. Though much more plot-driven than other Cirque shows, telling a complex saga about two Asian twins – supposedly a boy and a girl, but confusingly played by two women – who have been separated by enemy kidnappers, it's still basically a succession of truly breathtaking set-pieces. The maneuverability of the stage itself allows for some staggering aerial battles, and there's an astonishing "Wheel of Death" routine. Add in some extraordinary puppetry and sumptuous costumes, plus the artful use of fire and fog to conceal its mysteries, and even if you're left unmoved by the story, *Kà* is certain to expand your horizons.

La Femme

MGM Grand, 3799 Las Vegas Blvd S ☎702/891-7777. Daily except Tues 8pm & 10.30pm; all shows over-21s only. $59. Considering that *La Femme* is still claiming to be the latest thing in nude cabaret – imported in 2001 from the *Crazy Horse* in Paris, and installed near the front of the MGM Grand – it feels oddly like a silent movie or Victorian parlor game. The small stage plays host to a succession of rather static, self-consciously "arty" tableaux, in which not-very-naked women sing breathy songs about "paroxysmes d'erotisme" and the like, to be met by polite applause from an upscale audience who can be heard muttering about the high ticket prices during each plodding scene change. As so often, the best feature is the comedy interlude, in which the Quiddlers present the fabulous musical spoof "Micro Jackson."

Lance Burton

The Monte Carlo, 3770 Las Vegas Blvd S ☎702/730-7160. Tues & Sat 7pm & 10pm, Wed–Fri 7pm. $66 & $73. In 1996, the Monte Carlo lured master magician Lance Burton with a thirteen-year contract to direct and star in his own purpose-built 1200-seat theater. It was money well spent; Burton is a superb and charming performer, who accompanies stunning sleight of hand with patter delivered in his gentle Kentucky drawl. If no longer quite as young-looking as his publicity photos, he remains energetic and likeable. Most of the show consists of traditional but nevertheless impressive stunts with playing cards, handkerchiefs, and doves, but he also features large-scale illusions like the disappearance of an entire airplane and a narrow escape from hanging. With plenty of kids' participation too, it's the best family show in Las Vegas.

Showgirls of Magic

San Remo, 115 E Tropicana Ave ☎702/567-6028. Tues–Sun 8pm &

▲ TOURNAMENT OF KINGS

11.30pm; all shows over-18s only. $39, includes two drinks.

This enjoyable, old-fashioned revue occupies the tiny 120-seat showroom of the San Remo casino, located behind the Tropicana and across from the MGM Grand. Five leggy and intermittently topless showgirls dressed in red PVC hotpants perform basic but entertaining magic tricks, simultaneously and individually, with repeated interruptions for other impersonators, comedians, and magicians to do five- or ten-minute turns. The precise cast changes regularly – in essence, it's an audition show for the bigger-name revues elsewhere – but much of it tends to be hilarious.

Tournament of Kings

Excalibur, 3850 Las Vegas Blvd S ☎702/597-7600. Daily 6pm & 8.30pm. $53, including dinner. Excalibur can always be relied upon to know which side its bread is buttered; if the kids are happy, then everyone's happy. The *Tournament* is a twice-nightly piece of mock-medieval slapstick and schlockery, centering on a jousting match between a bad black knight and a good white knight that's accompanied by a great deal of tumbling, acrobatics, and

hell-raising audience participation, plus the chance to devour a Cornish game hen without the benefit of silverware. It's top-notch family fun, though clearly more directed at the younger set.

Zumanity

New York–New York, 3790 Las Vegas Blvd S ☎702/740-6815 or 866/606-7111, ⊛www.zumanity.com. Fri–Tues 7.30pm & 10.30pm; all shows over-18s only. $65–95, or $125 per person for a "duo sofa." In which everyone's favorite ethereal fantasists, the Cirque du Soleil, turn raunchy. Almost the first words are "Do you really want to see TITS?" – if you don't, you're in the wrong place. *Zumanity* has sharply divided audiences; some see it as a glorious celebration of human sexuality, others as a vulgar mishmash with only the odd hint of grace and beauty. There's certainly less acrobatic skill than in other Cirque shows, and thanks to a worthy intent to reflect all sizes and shapes, the displayed bodies tend to be less ravishing than you might expect. That the sex is inevitably stylized and simulated defuses the impact, but something here will almost certainly touch your buttons (literally, if you're sitting near the front). Ultimately, it's

▲ THE LITTLE CHURCH OF THE WEST

more accomplished than other topless revues, but if it's the Cirque du Soleil you want to see, catch their other Las Vegas shows first.

Shops

Las Vegas Outlet Center

7400 Las Vegas Blvd S ☏702/896-5599, ⓦwww.lasvegasoutletcenter .com. Mon–Sat 10am–10pm, Sun 10am–9pm. Though this ever-expanding, aesthetically challenged mall – located around three miles south of Mandalay Bay on the east side of Las Vegas Boulevard (no longer called the Strip by this point) – started life as a discount shopping center, its prices these days seem no cheaper than anywhere else. It is, however, easily accessible by car, and hosts over 150 stores, mostly clothing and footwear retailers like Levi's, Dress Barn, OshKosh B'Gosh, Nike Factory Store, and Reebok, plus the odd specialist store like Ritz Camera. While far from exciting, for everyday shopping, the Outlet Center provides a welcome alternative to the frenzy of the casino malls.

Mandalay Place

Mandalay Bay, 3930 Las Vegas Blvd S ☏702/632-7777. Sun–Thurs 10am–

11pm, Fri & Sat 10am–midnight. Though not on the scale of the Forum or the Grand Canal, Mandalay Bay's shopping mall, which lines the walkway connecting the casino with Luxor next door, does hold several unusual and interesting retailers, including the excellent Reading Room (the only genuine bookstore on the Strip), hipster clothing and lifestyle store Urban Outfitters, the stimulating Godt-Cleary Gallery, which specializes in big-name contemporary artists and designers, the first-ever Nike Golf store, and the Chocolate Swan, which sells exclusively chocolate desserts and pastries.

Wedding chapels

The Little Church of the West

4617 Las Vegas Blvd S ☏702/739-7971 or 800/821-2452, ⓦwww .littlechurchlv.com. Daily 8am–midnight. Built in 1942 and once part of the Last Frontier casino, this wedding chapel is now on the National Register of Historic Places and has moved progressively down the Strip over the years to its current site, south of Mandalay Bay. Among the more peaceful and quiet places to exchange your Vegas vows – if that's really what you want.

The Central Strip

The central section of the Strip remains the heart of Las Vegas. Bugsy Siegel's legendary Flamingo ruled the roost here from 1946 to 1966, when it was joined by Caesars Palace. Since then, more and more upstarts have arrived to keep these stalwarts on their mettle. After Bally's, originally the biggest hotel in the world, came the Mirage, which heralded the construction spree of the 1990s; then Bellagio, which set yet another new benchmark for luxury; and most recently the mighty Venetian. All stand within easy walking distance of the others, and with each forever unveiling its latest bid to outdo the rest, they all make essential stops on any Las Vegas itinerary.

The Aladdin

3667 Las Vegas Blvd S ☎ 702/785-5555, ⓦ www.aladdincasino.com.
Although it opened in August 2000 as Las Vegas's first mega-casino of the new millennium, the Aladdin actually represented the last gasp of the Strip's 1990s' construction boom. A lavish $1.4-billion project, it replaced its legendary namesake predecessor (1966–98), best known as the venue for Elvis and Priscilla's 1966 wedding. Sadly, however, the new Aladdin was beset by funding difficulties from the word go. Tipped into bankruptcy by the travel downturn that followed 9/11, it struggled on for three more years before being sold to Planet Hollywood. As this book went to press, the Aladdin was due to be completely redesigned and renamed **Planet Hollywood Hotel & Casino** when it opens again in the second half of 2006. With two performance spaces, and a partnership with music behemoth Clear Channel, Planet Hollywood will likely be counting on big-name live shows to draw in customers, rather than tired movie memorabilia.

What's ironic is that the factors which kept the Aladdin unprofitable mean that it's actually quite a nice place. One fundamental flaw was that you could explore the gigantic Desert Passage mall, and get to and from the hotel rooms, without ever crossing the casino floor. This factor, combined with the overall lack of crowds, makes Aladdin a more pleasant experience than many casinos, but has its obvious business disadvantages. Planet Hollywood will almost certainly spoil the ambience somewhat as it bids to crank up the gambling revenues.

▲ DESERT PASSAGE MALL

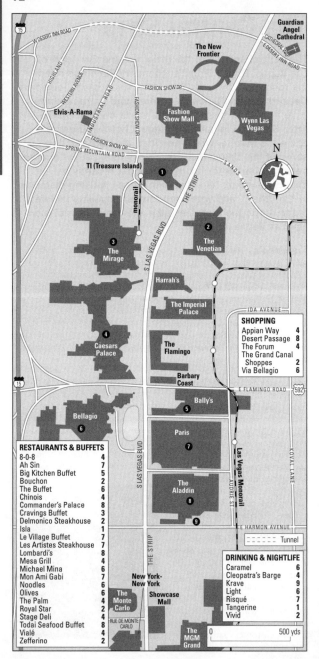

SHOPPING

Appian Way	4
Desert Passage	8
The Forum	4
The Grand Canal Shoppes	2
Via Bellagio	6

RESTAURANTS & BUFFETS

8-0-8	4
Ah Sin	7
Big Kitchen Buffet	5
Bouchon	2
The Buffet	6
Chinois	4
Commander's Palace	8
Cravings Buffet	3
Delmonico Steakhouse	2
Isla	1
Le Village Buffet	7
Les Artistes Steakhouse	7
Lombardi's	8
Mesa Grill	4
Michael Mina	6
Mon Ami Gabi	7
Noodles	6
Olives	6
The Palm	4
Royal Star	2
Stage Deli	4
Todai Seafood Buffet	8
Vialé	4
Zefferino	2

DRINKING & NIGHTLIFE

Caramel	6
Cleopatra's Barge	4
Krave	9
Light	6
Risqué	7
Tangerine	1
Vivid	2

0   500 yds

Currently, Aladdin's facade is designed to resemble a sort of lost city, perched on an artificial cliff and topped by an extravaganza of Moorish domes, while the casino within is bedecked with *Arabian Nights*–type flourishes – all of which will presumably disappear under more standard Vegas razzle-dazzle after the redesign.

At over a mile long, wrapped in a figure-eight around the Aladdin's casino and theater, the **Desert Passage** is a shopping mall on the same spectacular scale as the Forum and the Grand Canal Shoppes; its faux-blue "sky" even clouds over to deliver half-hourly "thunderstorms." Like the Aladdin as a whole, it will probably lose its Arabian theming, though that's less certain since it's under separate ownership from the casino itself.

Paris

3655 Las Vegas Blvd S ☎877/702-2096, ⓦwww.parislasvegas.com. By opening in September 1999, Paris, immediately north of the Aladdin, became the last Strip casino to be unveiled in the twentieth century. It's the handi-work of the same team that designed New York–New York, who operated under similar spatial constraints. To make the most of Paris's smallish site, they planted three legs of its center-piece Eiffel Tower replica smack in the middle of the casino floor, which is somewhat of a shame; feeling squashed up and claustrophobic is part of the fun of Manhattan, but Paris should surely be a bit more spacious and elegant.

It's slightly misleading to think of Paris as a separate casino at all, since it was originally built as a major extension to Bally's next door, to which it's linked by a broad corridor at the back. At $785 million, Paris cost around half as much as Bellagio or the Venetian, and it shares much of its infrastructure and management with Bally's. Time has gone by, however, and the tail is now clearly wagging the dog, with Bally's seen as a minor adjunct to Paris. The Strip-front exterior of Paris is a well-realized miniature, incorporating a welcome strolling and picture-taking area focused around the fourth leg of the Eiffel Tower, a sparkling fountain, a handful of trees, and a color-ful replica Montgolfier balloon. The joyful wealth of detail inside matches New York–New York, though in a slightly more twee and Disney-fied manner. Every member of staff (or "citizen of Paris") has a twenty-word French vocabulary, which is splendidly inadequate to cope with any genuine situation. Besides an assortment of top-notch French restaurants, you'll find authentic bakeries, pastry shops, and even toy stores where the *Sesame Street* dolls talk in French. As any true Parisian could have warned you, the cobbled alleyways wreak havoc on high heels, strollers, and wheeled suitcases, but no one seems too concerned. In the casino, a welcome air of Gallic

▼ EIFFEL TOWER, PARIS

glamour wafts over the gaming tables, which are covered by metalwork canopies modeled on Parisian metro stations. The theming falls apart completely, however, in the 1200-seat theater, now hosting the Queen musical, *We Will Rock You* – the casino's original plan to feature only French entertainment failed to pay off.

Standing 540ft tall, Paris's Eiffel Tower – officially, the **Eiffel Tower Experience** (daily 10am–midnight; $9) – is half the size of the original, and made of welded steel rather than wrought iron, with fake rivets added for cosmetic effect. Oddly enough, for all its presence on the Strip, the tower can barely be seen from elsewhere in the city. Nevertheless, taking the ninety-second ride straight through the casino roof and up to the summit – for which you

▲ LE NÔTRE PASTRY SHOP, PARIS

might have to wait in line for up to thirty minutes – offers amazing views, especially after dark, and most specifically across the Strip to Bellagio's water ballet. There's also a very expensive dinner-only restaurant, *La Tour Eiffel*, on the tower's first level.

Bally's

3645 Las Vegas Blvd S ☎ 888/742-9248, ⊛ www.ballyslv.com. Few visitors realize that Bally's casino started life in 1973 as the original MGM Grand. Entrepreneur Kirk Kerkorian had sold off almost the entire assets of MGM Studios to build the biggest hotel that had ever existed, named after the 1932 movie *Grand Hotel*. However, after it was devastated by fire in 1980 (see box below), Kerkorian sold the hotel to Bally's, the pinball and slot-machine manufacturers, retaining the MGM Grand name for future use.

Bally's status as one of the Strip's dullest buildings, consisting of little more than two monolithic towers of hotel rooms, has been only partially disguised by turning the whole thing into a giant neon sign. Not only the towers, but even the tubular walkway that carries

The MGM Grand fire

On the night of November 21, 1980, the casino now known as Bally's, but then called the MGM Grand, went from fame as the world's largest hotel to infamy as the site of Las Vegas's worst-ever hotel fire. Faulty wiring in the deli caused a blaze that's said to have engulfed the entire casino floor in just seven seconds. A total of 87 people died, with over 700 more injured.

Rumors spread of dire safety standards all along the Strip, and another fatal blaze (set by an arsonist) followed at the Hilton just two months later. Las Vegas at the time was already experiencing an economic downturn, with the (short-lived) emergence of Atlantic City, New Jersey, as a serious rival, and after the fires visitor numbers dropped even further. Nonetheless, the MGM Grand reopened within eight months, although with countless fire-related lawsuits still pending, owner Kirk Kerkorian chose to sell up within four years.

▲ MOVING WALKWAY AT BALLY'S

Strip pedestrians into the casino, shift constantly through a spectrum of four garish colors. Once inside, however, apart from the good-value *Big Kitchen Buffet*, there's little besides a run-of-the-mill casino, and most visitors head straight through to the Monorail station, right at the back of the property.

Bellagio

3600 Las Vegas Blvd S ☎ 888/987-6667, ⊕ www.bellagiolasvegas.com. Steve Wynn of Mirage Resorts set himself a very tall order when he started to plan Bellagio back in the mid-1990s. His goal was not to build merely the best hotel in Las Vegas – he felt he'd already done that with the Mirage – but the best hotel there has ever been, anywhere, outclassing even the legendary nineteenth-century *Ritz* in Paris. Before Bellagio, the theming in Las Vegas casinos was always playful – Luxor wasn't really a match for ancient Egypt, it just had fun pretending. Bellagio took itself more seriously. No longer was it enough to create an illusion; Bellagio, rather self-defeatingly, wanted to be somehow even better and more authentic than the Italian lakeside village for which it was named. The obvious trouble with this plan was that Bellagio is not in Europe, it's in Las Vegas, and stuffed full of slot machines – inlaid with jewel-like precision

into marble counters, perhaps, but slot machines nonetheless.

Nevertheless, when it opened in 1998, Bellagio was immediately recognized as being a quantum leap ahead of all its Las Vegas competitors, and quickly assumed an iconic status. Although its sheer opulence remains unmatched, the Venetian has since proved that you can be this classy without being quite so elitist, and combine grandeur with crowd-pleasing attractions and even a bit of old-style playfulness. Now, with Wynn himself gone (Mirage Resorts was bought by MGM in 2000), Bellagio could ultimately find itself outclassed by his newest creation, Wynn Las Vegas.

Bellagio's main hotel block, a stately curve of blue and cream pastels, stands aloof from the Strip behind an eight-acre replica of Italy's Lake Como. The mere presence of so much water in the desert announces Bellagio's extravagant wealth, but the point is rubbed in every half-hour, when submerged fountains erupt in water ballets, choreographed with booming music and colored lights.

Most pedestrians approach Bellagio from its northeast corner, crossing the bridges from Caesars Palace or Bally's. Ponderous mosaic-floored revolving doors grant admittance not to the usual moving walkway but to **Via Bellagio**, a plush paisley-carpeted mall of impossibly glamorous designer boutiques.

Hotel guests, by contrast, sweep up along a grand waterfront drive, to enter a sumptuous lobby where mosaic butterflies and insects writhe across the floor, and the ceiling is filled by a massively overblown chandelier

▲ BELLAGIO

of glass flowers, made by sculptor Dale Chihuly. The lobby leads in turn to the opulent **Conservatory**, where, beneath a Belle Epoque canopy of copper-framed glass, a network of flowerbeds is replanted every six to eight weeks with ornate seasonal displays.

To get the full benefit of Bellagio's facilities, which include a luxurious spa and beauty salon, and six superb swimming pools, you need to stay at the hotel. But the property as a whole is still an essential port of call for any visitor to Las Vegas. Even once you're done swooning over the general air of decadent luxury, there's still plenty to enjoy, including the stellar Cirque du Soleil show O, and the dozen or so top-quality restaurants, not to mention the best buffet in town.

The most conspicuous casualty of MGM's takeover of Bellagio has been the **Bellagio Gallery of Fine Art** (daily 9am–9pm; ⓦwww.bgfa.biz; $15), near the pool at the rear. Wynn's pride and joy formerly housed his personal portfolio of Picassos and Monets, and was seen (by him more than anyone else), as a bold attempt to introduce high culture to the Las Vegas scene.

Now significantly outclassed by the Venetian's Guggenheim, the small, overpriced gallery simply features temporary and often lackluster exhibitions.

Caesars Palace

3570 Las Vegas Blvd S ☎877/427-7243, ⓦwww.caesars.com. Despite approaching its fortieth birthday – a venerable age by Las Vegas standards – Caesars Palace remains the most famous name in the casino business. In the last few years, it has comprehensively overhauled itself to meet the challenge of upstart rivals like Bellagio and the Venetian, and is now once again a mustsee for every visitor.

Las Vegas's definitive themed casino was unveiled in 1966. Costing under $25 million to build – less than the volcano at the Mirage – it was the brainchild of entrepreneur Jay Sarno, and the first Vegas casino to be financed through loans from the pension fund of Jimmy Hoffa's Teamsters' Union. A powerful Mob presence was barely concealed from the word go, and became even more apparent after Sarno sold out in 1969, but Caesars has been under sanitized corporate control since the early 1980s.

Caesars was originally designed to be approached by car, its distance from the highway making it seem even more majestic. When pedestrians started to cruise the Strip, Caesars was the first casino to

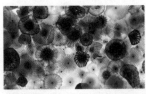

▲ CHIHULY SCULPTURE, BELLAGIO LOBBY

respond by constructing moving walkways to haul them in – and it also established the tradition of making it as hard as possible for them to get out again.

Sarno's crucial legacy lay in setting the place up on an expanse of land that has so far proved big enough to hold every enlargement architects have been able to imagine. Most recent construction has been aimed at filling the space in front of the casino proper, to give it a more intimate connection with the Strip. The original trademark Italianate fountains are still there, but they've been joined by an ever-expanding array of pseudo-classical statuary and pavilions, as well as the towering circular **Colosseum**, and an open-air **Roman Plaza** that's a daring attempt to introduce cafe society to the heart of the Strip, and even features an open-air boxing arena.

Even though Caesars remains relatively "small" in terms of hotel space, its interior is a bewildering labyrinth, vast enough that it can take half an hour's brisk walk to get from one end to the other. And that's if you know the place well; with its low ceilings, low lights, and lack of signs, it's designed to be as disorienting as possible, and you're all too likely to be distracted by the appearance of a Cleopatra-cropped cocktail waitress, or an armor-clad Roman legionary standing guard atop a bank of slot machines.

Caesars has been renowned for big-name **entertainment** ever since 1967, when it secured the services of Frank Sinatra for $100,000 a week. While its heyday as a Rat Pack

hangout came to an abrupt end when Sinatra and an executive vice-president exchanged blows on the casino floor while discussing a baccarat debt, the tradition of A-list performers is being maintained by the long-term residencies of Celine Dion and Elton John in the Colosseum. Although Caesars was also for many years the city's premier boxing venue, since the 1990s that role has been taken in turn by the Mirage, the MGM Grand, and Mandalay Bay.

A high proportion of visitors to Caesars come to explore the hugely successful **Forum** mall, with its top-notch collection of restaurants and stores. Ever since it opened in 1992, crowds have gathered to gawk at the complex play of lights which transforms its blue-domed, cloud-strewn ceiling between dawn and dusk every hour, and new enhancements and extensions have been added at regular intervals. Ornate fountains at either end are peopled by gloriously kitsch animatronic statues that come to life at regular intervals – one represents the

▲ THE FORUM

▲ BARBARY COAST

sunken kingdom of Atlantis – while an artificial moon now waxes and wanes above the central Fountain of the Gods.

Barbary Coast

3595 Las Vegas Blvd S ☎ 888/227-2279, ⓦ www.barbarycoastcasino.com. Slotted in between so many Strip behemoths, the tiny, 200-room Barbary Coast feels like a throwback to a long-lost Las Vegas. Its main distinguishing feature is a classic piece of old Vegas neon, the hourglass-shaped sign above its front entrance. That entrance is always thrown open, and with clattering tables and slots just inside, the Barbary Coast is kept ticking along nicely by walk-in gamblers weary of ogling its outsized neighbors.

The interior of the Barbary Coast is filled with brass and glass, including "the world's largest Tiffany-style glass mural." Amenities on the ground floor, however, are minimal. Apart from the chilled shrimp cocktails behind the main bar, there isn't even any food on sale, though inconspicuous elevators lead to a pair of expensive restaurants, *Drai's* and *Michael's*.

The Flamingo

3555 Las Vegas Blvd S ☎ 888/308-8899, ⓦ www.flamingolasvegas.com. Though neither brick nor bloodstain remains of the original resort, the very name of the Flamingo is dripping with Las Vegas legend. Still widely thought of as the first of the great Strip casinos, El Rancho Vegas and the Last Frontier were actually already here when it opened in 1946, and the Flamingo was originally more of a stylish motel than a neon extravaganza. It was the creation of New York mobster Benjamin "don't call me Bugsy" Siegel, who paid the ultimate price for opening the incomplete casino slightly too early in desperation to start repaying the enormous loans he took out to build it. The Flamingo closed down after only two weeks, leaving Siegel even deeper in debt. Although it swiftly reopened, Siegel's backers had by that point lost patience, and he was shot dead in June 1947.

In a sense, Siegel's death was the perfect advertising gimmick, as it turned out Las Vegas punters actually liked to feel that they were rubbing shoulders with murderous gangsters. It took countless changes of ownership before the Mob presence was finally shucked off, and the Flamingo is now part of the Caesars empire. Today, it stakes its patch opposite Caesars with

▲ THE FLAMINGO

a magnificent cascade of neon,
centering on a bulbous unfurl-
ing flower of light. As recently as
1990, this was the largest hotel
in the world; now it pitches
itself (not entirely convincingly)
as a sophisticated upmarket
resort, an elder statesman too
secure of its status to have to
bother competing head-on
with brash modern competitors.
Only a continuing design predilection for the kind of pinks
and oranges seldom seen outside
Barbie's boudoir bear witness to
the Flamingo's racy past.

Although there's little to see
or do in the casino proper, the
landscaped **Wildlife Habitat
and Arboretum** around the
back is a lovely garden complex
of pools, lagoons, water slides,
palm-shaded walkways, and
abundant flamingos, both real
and plastic. There are also a few
African penguins, unique among
their kind in having adapted to
hot climates.

The Imperial Palace

3535 Las Vegas Blvd S ☎800/634-
6441, ⊛www.imperialpalace.com.
Dragons or not, the ultra-tacky
checkered exterior of the Imperial Palace looks less like the
facade of a major casino than
that of a rundown used-car
dealership – which in a sense
it is (see below). Nonetheless,
this is among Las Vegas's largest
hotels, and every square inch of
the twelve-acre site that stretches
away from its slender frontage
on the Strip is pressed into use.
It has even built over its driveway, so when you stroll off the
Strip into what you expect to
be the casino, you quickly find
yourself either outdoors again,
or dropping beneath it on an
elaborate escalator system.

The emphasis at the Imperial
remains squarely on gambling.

▲ THE IMPERIAL PALACE

As well as having a splendidly
old-fashioned **Race Book**,
rising in tiers above a central
pit, the Imperial also hosts a
frenzied daily slot tournament,
"Wild Times." In one section
of the casino floor, celebrity
lookalike "dealertainers" help
to promote the on-site *Legends*
show.

Former Imperial owner Ralph
Engelstad, who died in 2001,
had a predilection for dictators
(he was once fined $1.5 million
by the Nevada Gaming Control
Board for holding a party to
celebrate Hitler's birthday) and a
passion for cars. **The Auto
Collections** (daily 9.30am–
9.30pm; ⊛www.autocollections
.com; $7, free with coupon from
casino or listings magazines) can
still be visited on the fifth floor
of the parking garage at the
rear, though many of Engelstad's
personal favorites are now gone,
as every vehicle is up for sale.
Among the few with celebrity
connections that remain are a
1959 Cadillac used by Marilyn
Monroe, and Steve McQueen's
Big Chief motorcycle. Prices
range from $9800 for a 1977

Chrysler to $3 million for a 1961 Aston Martin, while the oldest car on display dates from 1922.

Harrah's

3475 Las Vegas Blvd S ☎702/369-5000, ⓦwww.harrahsvegas.com. Until 1997, Harrah's was one of Las Vegas's best-known landmarks, kitted out as a proud, neon-decked paddlewheeler and known as the "Ship on the Strip." Spurred to upgrade by the proximity of mega-rivals like the Mirage and Caesars Palace, however, it then ditched the supposedly old-fashioned riverboat trimmings in favor of a bland, unoriginal carnival theme. Gone too are the "party pits" in the casino, where the dealers dressed in party hats and capered like loons. Its frontage now festooned with trumpeting Mardi Gras jesters, Harrah's is actually a sedate, rather boring joint, enlivened only (if at all) by the open-air performances on the Carnaval Court plaza at its southern end. Inside, Harrah's caters to its middle-aged clientele by making everything easy to find, and teases them with a prominent statue of "The Greenbacks," a lifelike tourist couple dripping dollars from every pore and pocket.

Harrah's is so outmatched by the competition that even if its parent company's $9.4 billion bid to buy the entire Caesars operation (including Caesars Palace, Paris, Bally's, and the Flamingo) goes through – the purchase had yet to be finalized by the time this book went to press – their flagship casino will surely remain something of a poor relation.

The Mirage

3400 Las Vegas Blvd S ☎800/374-9000, ⓦwww.mirage.com. Perhaps the best measure of the impact of the Mirage upon Las Vegas is that it's become hard to remember quite what was so different about the place. When Steve Wynn built it in 1989, he eschewed many time-honored Las Vegas traditions, lavishing unprecedented amounts of money on fixtures and fittings for the guest rooms, and plating the entire facade with 24-carat gold stripes. Though the success of Wynn's $620 million gamble transformed the city, in due course Bellagio relegated the Mirage to second-best even within the Mirage Resorts chain. These days, it no longer stands out from the crowd, and guests who once stayed here as a matter of course can now choose from a dozen other top-rank alternatives.

One of Wynn's radical innovations with the Mirage lay in recognizing that increased pedestrian traffic on the Strip called for a new kind of architecture. Hence the much-vaunted **"volcano"** outside, created to lure tourists out onto the Strip

▲ THE MIRAGE

at night, and then into the casino itself. Basically a lumpy fiberglass island, topped by palm trees and poking from a shallow artificial lagoon, it "erupts" in genteel cascades of water and flame every fifteen minutes between nightfall and midnight. It would be hard to imagine anything that was less like a volcano, but for many years jostling crowds nonetheless filled the sidewalk to catch a peek – though the novelty finally seems to be wearing off.

The volcano also serves to signal the tropical theme of the Mirage, not that you'll need reminding if you go inside. Entering its opulent atrium, housed beneath a geodesic dome, feels like stepping into a lush garden, while a giant fish tank behind the registration desks teems with pygmy sharks and stingrays. For non-gamblers, though, the Mirage offers less to see and do than the newer mega-casinos, and it can't match the top-notch restaurants found in places like Caesars, the Venetian, or Bellagio.

The big question hanging over the place, however, is how it will redefine itself now that illusionists **Siegfried and Roy** have gone. The Teutonic duo were synonymous with the Mirage until an October 2003 incident, in which Roy Horn was nearly killed by one of the white tigers, abruptly closed their show forever. An even more prestigious double act has been lined up to follow them, however, with the opening in 2006 of a new Cirque du Soleil show based on the music of the Beatles.

At the time of writing, you could usually still see one or two of Siegfried and Roy's trademark white tigers for free,

▲ SECRET GARDEN AND DOLPHIN HABITAT

in a glassed-in environment alongside the main entrance. For a more fulfilling experience, pay to enter the **Secret Garden and Dolphin Habitat** (Mon–Fri 11am–5.30pm, Sat & Sun 10am–5.30pm; $12, under-10s free), near the pool area at the back of the property. This surprisingly spacious zoo – a better deal than Mandalay Bay's Shark Reef (see p.53) – is divided into two distinct parts. The first consists of two interconnected pools, in which you can watch dolphins "exercise" (as opposed to performing tricks, though it comes to much the same thing) both above and below the water. Enclosures beyond hold the world's greatest concentration of big white cats, including snow leopards and heterozygous white lions, all given names like "Destiny." Siegfried and/or Roy continue to regale visitors with soporific anecdotes via "audio wands."

TI

3300 Las Vegas Blvd S ☎ 800/288-7206, ⊛ www.treasureisland.com. No casino epitomizes the way Las Vegas has changed in the last dozen years quite so perfectly as TI (Treasure Island). When it was built by Mirage Enterprises

▲ TI

has been revamped as a "sexy" adult show, in which the victorious ship is now crewed by the scantily-clad **Sirens of TI**, who screech rock songs to lure the few remaining pirates into their clutches (nightly 7pm, 8.30pm, 10pm & 11.30pm).

in 1993, using the first flush of profits from the Mirage next door (to which it's still connected by a standalone monorail link), the city was in thrall to the notion that it was about to become a child-friendly destination to rank alongside Orlando, Florida. Hence Treasure Island, which took the Mirage's volcano concept several stages further by having its entire lower facade sculpted into a novelty attraction – an intricate, pastel-pretty seafront village that's obviously modeled on Disney's *Pirates of the Caribbean* ride. Amid much yo-ho-ho-ing and cannonfire, two "pirate ships" clashed nightly on the moat in front, drawing crowds of kids and their parents to the boardwalks and rigging that line the Strip sidewalk.

When MGM took over the Mirage empire in 2000, however, they hastened to abandon the very idea of appealing to children. All Treasure Island's lovingly crafted fripperies have been stripped away, from its huge video arcade and bizarre $400,000 bone chandeliers, to the skull motifs that adorned everything from its main sign to the doorhandles. Even its very name has gone, replaced by the anodyne acronym TI. And most ludicrous of it all, the pirate battle

Treasure Island always catered very cannily to its yuppie clientele, most notably by hosting the city's best production show, the Cirque du Soleil's *Mystère*, so the changes inside have not needed to be so crass or dramatic. Also, while there might not be much here in the way of attractions, TI's bars and restaurants have been nicely upgraded, the pool and spa are excellent, and there's a very high-tech Race and Sports Book.

The Venetian

3265 Las Vegas Blvd S ☎877/883-6423, ⓦwww.venetian.com.
The brainchild of Sheldon Adelson – who made his fortune establishing Las Vegas's COMDEX exhibition as the world's premier computer trade show – the Venetian occupies the fabled spot where the old Rat Pack haunt, the Sands casino, stood from 1952 to 1996.

The birth of the Venetian was plagued with complications, and its eventual emergence in 1999, with only a handful of restaurants in action and no shops, was acclaimed as a textbook example of how *not* to open a casino. Initial prognostications were gloomy, and it racked up heavy losses. A few years on, however, it has become a major success story. While lavish enough to match Bellagio, it's much more user-friendly, with architecture and attractions to lure in passing tourists, and the convention center and upscale accommodation to keep it packed with business travelers. The opening of the sumptuous Venezia tower in 2003 took the Venetian's total to over four thousand rooms, while another three-thousand-room tower is likely to appear during the lifetime of this book. Until 2005, entertainment was the one weak link, and that too has now been addressed with the transfer from Luxor of the Blue Man Group, and the 2006 arrival of the *Phantom of the Opera* for a long-term run in its own theater.

Mr Adelson's dream was apparently to cram all the snapshots of his real-life honeymoon in Venice, Italy, within a single frame. The Venetian's Strip facade incorporates facsimiles of six major Venice buildings – from south to north, the Library, the Campanile, the Palazzo Contarini-Fasan, the Doge's Palace, the Ca' d'Oro, and the Clock Tower – as well as the Rialto Bridge, the Bridge of Sighs, and a small stretch of "canal." In front of them all stand two massive columns, modeled on a pair brought to Venice from Constantinople in 1172. As the originals were used for public executions, superstitious Venetians avoid passing between them to this day. In Las Vegas, however, there's little choice – they flank the main casino entrance.

The internal layout of the Venetian focuses around extravagant public spaces like the huge hallway that leads to the hotel lobby, paved with Escher-like *trompe l'oeil* marble tiles, and the magnificent central stairwell, topped by vivid frescoes, that

leads to the breathtaking **Grand Canal**. This preposterous re-creation of the waterways of Venice, complete with gondolas and opera-singing gondoliers, is quintessential Las Vegas, and as such utterly irresistible – for God's sake, most of it is *upstairs*. Topped by a Forum-esque fake sky, it's lined by the **Grand Canal Shoppes**. A store at the far end sells tickets for gondola rides, both inside and also the section of canal outside (indoors Sun–Thurs 10am–11pm, Fri & Sat 10am–midnight, outdoors much shorter hours, varying seasonally; $12 per person, $5 under-12s, or $50 for a two-person private ride).

As for Strip-level attractions, in 2001, the Venetian upstaged Bellagio by opening two distinct Guggenheim art museums, though only the smaller **Guggenheim Hermitage** (daily 9am–8.30pm; Ⓦ www.guggenheimlasvegas.org; $15, under-13s $7), just off the lobby, has survived. This earns much-needed funds for St Petersburg's State Hermitage Museum by displaying its finest treasures on a changing rotation. Exhibitions tend to concentrate on Impressionism and Cubism, with Monet, Picasso, and Van

▼ THE VENETIAN

Gogh well represented. As the four rooms typically only hold around thirty paintings at a time, you may feel the price is high, but there's no disputing the quality of the works.

The Venetian's other major attraction is the first US outpost of **Madame Tussaud's** waxwork museum (daily 10am–10pm, some seasonal variation; ⓦwww.mtvegas.com; $20, under-13s $10). Set on the second and third floors of the Library, it's styled as "Interactive Wax," on the grounds that visitors can shoot hoops with Shaq, sink a putt with Tiger, or sing karaoke for Simon Cowell. As for most of the effigies, however, you can merely pose for photographs with them, prod them gently, or make sarcastic remarks about them. Unless you've always dreamed of shaking hands with a wax model of chef Wolfgang Puck, you may well feel the whole experience seriously overpriced.

Restaurants

8-0-8

Caesars Palace, 3570 Las Vegas Blvd S ☎702/731-7110. Dinner only, closed Tues & Wed. Located just off Caesars' main lobby, Hawaiian superchef Jean-Marie Josselin's sparsely adorned *8-0-8* (named for Hawaii's area code) specializes in a fusion of Asian and European cuisines that's best represented with superb $14–25 appetizers like crab cakes with spicy remoulade and Josselin's trademark "deconstructed *ahi* roll." Meat entrees tend to be fairly conventional, such as a roasted free-range chicken ($26) or seared New York strip ($36), albeit served with more exotic vegetables like red lentil dahl or

a shiitake mushroom compote. As for seafood, the emphasis is on Hawaiian fish like wok-charred *mahi mahi* ($24) or bamboo-steamed *opakapaka* ($28). For a real treat, try the changing $79 "Taste of Hawaii" tasting menu. For desserts, the accent becomes firmly French, with fabulous soufflés.

Ah Sin

Paris, 3655 Las Vegas Blvd S ☎702/946-7000. This large and lavish pan-Asian restaurant, right at the front of Paris, sets out to be all things to all diners, serving a full menu of dishes from all over Asia. It offers a wide choice of where to sit, not only on an outdoor patio on the Strip or the glitzy high-tech dining room, but also at a Malaysian satay bar or a sushi bar. You can even enjoy *Ah Sin*'s rich French desserts in the attached *Risqué* lounge/nightclub upstairs. On the whole the food is good rather than exceptional, but with so much choice you're bound to find a favorite. A plate of their signature Ah Sin fried rice, a Cantonese crêpe, or a *char siu* bun will cost under $10, and a small-ish mixed sushi or sashimi combo under $15, while prices for fancier entrees like barbecue suckling pig range ever upwards.

Bouchon

Venezia Tower, The Venetian, 3355 Las Vegas Blvd S ☎702/414-6200. Despite its sky-high reputation and exclusive setting – just off the ornate tenth-floor lobby of the Venetian's Venezia Tower – Thomas Keller's spacious re-creation of a classic French bistro (the much smaller original is in Napa Valley) is both friendly and affordable. The interior design is meticulously authentic, but the real joy here is to sit outside on the huge open piazza that spreads beneath the hotel towers; there's no view of the Strip, but the sky is magnificent (and uncannily like the faux sky of the Forum at sunset). *Bouchon*'s every dish is prepared with perfect precision, and the prices are surprisingly reasonable, with a delicious French onion soup for $8.50 and a flavorful roast chicken with onions and garlic at $22.50. There's also plenty of seafood, like oysters and mussels. Breakfast is a Francophile's dream of croissants, pastries, yogurt, and coffee.

Chinois

Forum Shops, Caesars Palace, 3570 Las Vegas Blvd S ☎702/737-9700. Wolfgang Puck's postmodern Asian-fusion restaurant offers cafe-style terrace seating at the Forum's mall level, and a more formal dining room upstairs. *Chinois'* decor is stylish – all tiles, jade, and turquoise, with running water to aid the *feng shui* – but the tables themselves are kept minimal, with no tablecloths, ornaments, or even condiments, and the young black-clad staff can be too busy posing glamorously to provide attentive service. The food itself is upmarket, nouvelle-tinged, and mostly Chinese. Appetizers ($7–10) include pork potstickers and stir-fried chicken lettuce wraps – while entrees ($22–31) range from sizzling catfish via roast duck to Shanghai lobster. Good-value, three-course set lunches cost $13–15.

Commander's Palace

Desert Passage, Aladdin, 3663 Las Vegas Blvd S ☎702/892-8272, ⓦwww.commanderspalace.com.

New Orleans' renowned haute Creole restaurant – repeatedly voted the best restaurant in the US – occupies pride of place at the front of the Desert Passage, with its windows facing right on the Strip. The dark wood fittings, and combination of formal place settings with friendly service, do a great job of evoking the Big Easy, though at $7.50 for a bowl of gumbo the prices can come as a shock. From classic appetizers like shrimp remoulade ($10.50), through entrees such as pecan-crusted Gulf fish ($29) or veal chop Tchoupitoulas ($39), to a dessert of Bananas Foster ($7.50) – invented by the Brennan family, who have owned *Commander's* for over a century – it's a gourmet's delight. The three-course set dinner is $39, but for a complete blow-out, opt for the $85 seven-course tasting menu. There's also a $35 champagne jazz brunch on Friday, Saturday, or Sunday.

Delmonico Steakhouse

The Venetian, 3355 Las Vegas Blvd S ☎702/414-3737. Although TV chef Emeril Lagasse has given Las Vegas a classic New Orleans steakhouse with *Delmonico*, the decor is "modern Tuscan," in deference to the Venetian's Italian roots. Only one of its

▼ BOUCHON

PLACES The Central Strip

many dining rooms, equipped with arched ceilings and a fireplace, is at all intimate or appealing; the rest are austere and minimal, and overall it's much more refined than Emeril's raucous *Fish House* at the MGM Grand. The whole place reeks of money: a humble baked potato costs $6.50, while several wines hit the $3000 mark. Even the least likely items come swimming in butter – Emeril's not one to stint – but the meat at the core of the experience is excellent, with each large and very tender steak priced at $34–44. While there's usually just one fish entree, such as a $27 grilled salmon, appetizers include barbecue shrimp at $10.50 and oysters Bienville for $12. Lunch consists of smaller, cheaper servings of substantially the same menu.

Isla

TI, 3300 Las Vegas Blvd S ☎702/894-7111. A lot of people pass quickly through this high-class, good-value Mexican restaurant, pausing for a hasty snack or swift shot, but there's much to savor if you choose to linger. Besides the expected $12 enchiladas and $16 tostadas, chef Richard Sandoval's open kitchen – set in a dramatic wall of stunning blue *azulejo* tiles – serves up imaginative, tasty specialties that range from

home-style Mexican meatballs for $14 up to grilled filet mignon for $32. Be sure to sample an appetizer like the trio of crunchy corn masa cakes with different toppings for $7, or the $14 warm seafood salad. The large tequila bar offers around 75 varieties by the glass, from $5.50 up to $30.

Les Artistes Steakhouse

Paris, 3655 Las Vegas Blvd S ☎702/967-7999. Dinner only. Stylish, elegantly modern European-style grand cafe, set on two levels in the heart of Paris, and serving high-quality French bistro cuisine with a modern Asian twist. From the mosaics and Monet-inspired upholstery, to the graceful double staircase that swirls up toward the Belle Epoque ceiling, the atmosphere is just right. The best of the appetizers are the traditional onion soup ($7.50) and a duck *cassoulette* tart ($13); entrees range from lemon pepper chicken ($19) to seared *ahi* tuna ($26) and filet mignon ($39); and the dessert pastries are out of this world.

Lombardi's

Desert Passage, Aladdin, 3663 Las Vegas Blvd S ☎702/731-1755. Dependable, good-value Italian restaurant, with seating both indoors and "outdoors" (under the artificial sky) in the Desert Passage's appealing Oasis Square, with its revolving cast of street musicians, acrobats, and belly dancers. *Lombardi's* offers pretty much all things to all comers, whether you fancy a soup or salad for $6–8, a cheap pasta or pizza meal for $12–16, or a gourmet special such as veal piccata or sea bass in lemon butter for $20–25. Similarly, tables come

▲ LES ARTISTES STEAKHOUSE

with paper tablecloths and crayons, so the kids can doodle, but there's a stylish flourish to the service to ensure that the adults will feel catered to.

▲ NOODLES

Mesa Grill

Caesars Palace, 3570 Las Vegas Blvd S ☎702/731-7731. Dinner only. Serving contemporary Southwestern cuisine in a prime location facing the Colosseum doors, Bobby Flay's stylish *Mesa Grill* is a heavyweight addition to Caesars' roster of gourmet restaurants. You're in for a flavorful treat; think crunchy cornmeal coatings and sharp chili accents. Appetizers, at $10–16, are heavily geared towards seafood, though there's also a goat cheese *queso fundido*. Entrees are generally $28–40, and include assorted steaks, crusted snappers, and a sumptuous pan-roasted rabbit served with yellow-tomato risotto.

Michael Mina

Bellagio, 3600 Las Vegas Blvd S ☎702/693-7223. Dinner only. This offshoot of the celebrated San Francisco seafood restaurant (formerly known as *Aqua*), in Bellagio's Conservatory, has established itself in Las Vegas's very highest dining echelon, with tasteful, understated decor that matches the exquisite delicacy of the cuisine. The standout appetizer is the $16 black mussel soufflé, while the zestful, $41, porcini-crusted turbot, served with scallop canelloni, is typical of the entrees. Rather strangely, the only alternative to seafood for carnivores is *foie gras*, with an entire roast one costing $95. If

you can't bear to decide, there are tasting menus for $85 and $115, with optional wine pairings, and a wholly vegetarian alternative at $70.

Mon Ami Gabi

Paris, 3655 Las Vegas Blvd S ☎702/944-4224. Las Vegas life doesn't get much better than lunch at *Mon Ami Gabi*, with its open-air seating right on the Strip, facing Bellagio's fountains and rendered comfortable by parasols in summer and outdoor heaters in winter. The feel is of a proper French pavement bistro, both outside and in the conservatory-like indoor dining room. As for the menu, it boasts a gloriously authentic onion soup ($7) that's buried so deep in cheese it's almost impossible to find; juicy *moules marinières* (mussels; $11); and thin-cut *steak frites* ($21). The choice expands for dinner, with other steak cuts such as *onglet* ("hanger steak"; $20); oysters or whatever shellfish is in season; and fresh fish entrees. End the meal with a fine, rich French dessert, such as *crêpe suzette* ($6–8).

Noodles

Bellagio, 3600 Las Vegas Blvd S ☎702/693-8131. Daily until 3am. Despite being hidden away behind the *Baccarat* bar and having a lower profile than Bellagio's big-name restaurants, this all-purpose Asian eatery is a stylish, high-class affair, kitted out like a postmodern apothecary with display shelves of slender glass jars. The surprisingly inexpensive menu spans Thai, Japanese, Vietnamese, and Chinese cuisine, with soup noodles at $10–16, wok-fried noodles $14–18, and similarly priced alternatives such as barbecued pork or duck, and steamed rice or congee. Of the dim sum, the $7 *shiu mai* dumplings, packed with minced pork and large pieces of shrimp, and served with a searing mustard sauce, are absolutely succulent.

Olives

Bellagio, 3600 Las Vegas Blvd S ☎702/693-7223. Modeled by Todd English and Victor LaPlaca on their Boston original, Bellagio's best-value gourmet restaurant has a lovely terrace setting, facing the Eiffel Tower across the lake. Only a few lucky diners get to sit out there; the rest have to make do with the more formal, elegant dining room indoors. Even if *Olives* is the kind of place that calls a $15 pizza an "individual oven-baked flatbread," and your food is more likely to be arranged vertically than horizontally, the largely Mediterranean menu is uniformly fresh and superb. It's a great spot for lunch, with $10–13 appetizers like tuna or beef carpaccio and slow-braised lamb ribs, pasta dishes like butternut squash tortelli ($16), and specials such as barbecued yellow-fin tuna on roasted-onion polenta with spicy avocado salad ($21.50). Dinner entrees are pricier, at $28–50, but at least you get their trademark platter

of huge, delicious olives as soon as you sit down.

The Palm

Forum Shops, Caesars Palace, 3500 Las Vegas Blvd S ☎702/732-7256. Classy, upmarket steakhouse near the Forum entrance, closely modeled on the New York power-dining original and festooned with caricatures of local celebrities. The food may not be all that exciting, cooked with a better-safe-than-sorry approach that can make it all pretty heavy, but it's somehow deeply reassuring, and the service is impeccable. At lunchtime, you can get a burger for $10 or a "Business Lunch" of soup or salad and steak for $17; for dinner, choose from five veal entrees at $22–25 each or get a full steak for $35–40.

Royal Star

The Venetian, 3355 Las Vegas Blvd S ☎702/414-1888. It may not sound quite high-concept enough to catch the eye in Las Vegas, but if you enjoy superlative Chinese cuisine – and unfashionably large portions – *Royal Star* is well worth seeking out. Taiwanese master-chef Kevin Wu specializes in seafood, so tanks in the kitchen are filled with fresh fish flown in daily from around the world, ready for succulent dishes like steamed giant shrimp or sea bass baked with tofu in a clay pot. The lengthy menu abounds in reasonably priced standards like roast duck with plum sauce for $19 or kung pao chicken at $18, plus appetizers such as a fabulous salt-and-pepper squid, but make sure to ask about daily specials. For dinner, the decor is smartly formal, with magnificent flower arrangements, and the ambience peaceful and unhurried, though things get more hectic at lunch-time when the dim-sum trolleys go scurrying through.

Stage Deli

Forum Shops, Caesars Palace, 3570 Las Vegas Blvd S ☎702/893-4045. Despite its checked floors and Formica tables, this outpost of New York's famous *Stage Deli* fails to look much like the original, but at least the food is straight out of New York. The main stock in trade is sandwiches, with a huge pile of pastrami on rye costing $9.50, and celebrity-named triple-deckers like the Wayne Newton (turkey and salami) or the Tom Jones (chicken salad) more like $11–13. If you can't manage all that bread, go for a combo special, and get half a sandwich plus a bowl of borscht and a bucket of pickles for about the same price.

Vialé

Roman Plaza, Caesars Palace, 3500 Las Vegas Blvd S ☎702/731-7110. Somehow, this inexpensive sidewalk Italian trattoria, right beside the Strip on Caesars' Roman Plaza, seems almost too good to be true. It's so unexpected to find a casino restaurant outdoors and away from the tables, that *Vialé* is often surprisingly empty. Which is a shame, because lunch beneath its black-and-white awnings is an absolute treat, with a burger or warm panini sandwich costing under $10, and a Caesar salad (well you would, wouldn't you?) for $7, or $10 with chicken. The dinner menu offers many of the same salads, plus pasta as both appetizer ($7–9) and entree ($12–17), and more substantial entrees like pan-seared halibut or grilled quail with mascarpone stuffing, both at $19. A takeout window sells pizza by the slice.

▲ VIALÉ

Zeffirino

Grand Canal Shoppes, The Venetian, 3355 Las Vegas Blvd S ☎702/414-3500. Though purists might not approve of the intrinsic fakery of the Venetian branch of this venerable Genoa restaurant, any Las Vegas aficionado just has to love it. It manages to be both very formal, even roman-tic, with its rich tapestries and curtains and meticulous silver service, but yet playful, with ornate balconies overlooking the Grand Canal and the songs of the gondoliers wafting up. Dinner entrees can be pricey, with a basic ravioli at $26 and fish dishes at $26–40, but the $20 three-course set lunch (served daily except Sundays) is an exceptional value. Sunday sees a $45 champagne "gourmet brunch," featuring lobsters, oysters, and Chateaubriand.

Buffets

Big Kitchen Buffet

Bally's, 3645 Las Vegas Blvd S ☎702/739-4111. Breakfast $11, lunch $13, dinner $18. For dinner, Bally's *Big Kitchen* – reached by making

▲ CRAVINGS BUFFET

a sharp right as soon as you enter the casino from the Strip – ranks among the better old-style buffets, offering a comprehensive spread of fresh meats and seafood (including shrimp at lunchtime, and substantial casseroles and stews at dinner) plus a wide-ranging salad bar. Other than a few Chinese dinner entrees, however, the selection is all rather homogeneous. The *Big Kitchen* is not to be confused with Bally's *Champagne Sterling Brunch*, served in a separate room on Sundays (9.30am–2.30pm), where the roast meats and seafood (including lobster, caviar, and sashimi) are all magnificent – as indeed they should be for $58.

The Buffet

Bellagio, 3600 Las Vegas Blvd S
☎702-791-7111. Breakfast Mon–Fri $14; brunch Sat & Sun $22, or $28 with champagne; lunch Mon–Fri $18; dinner Sun–Fri $26, Sat $34. Far and away Las Vegas's best buffet – assuming price is not an issue. With other buffets, you may rave about what good value they are; with Bellagio's, you'll rave about what good food it serves. The high cost keeps the crowds relatively thin, and the lines are never too long. While the large dining area is not especially attractive, it offers spacious seating; there are even restrooms inside, an astounding innovation. At 800

items, all prepared fresh in small quantities, the sheer range of food is extraordinary. For breakfast, besides the expected bagels, pastries, and eggs, you can have salmon smoked or baked, fruit fresh or in salads, and omelets cooked to order, with fillings such as crabmeat. Lunch offerings can include sushi, cold cuts, dim sum, barbecued wild boar ribs and lamb *osso bucco*, plus fresh-baked *focaccia*, tasty fruit tarts, figs and grapes, and fancy desserts. Dinner is similar, but the stakes are raised again with the addition of entrees like lobster claws, fresh oysters, and venison.

Cravings Buffet

The Mirage, 3400 Las Vegas Blvd S
☎702-792-7777. Breakfast $12.50, lunch $17.50, dinner $22.50. It may not quite live up to its billing as "the ultimate buffet dining experience," but the re-vamped and re-named buffet at the Mirage certainly provides a few new twists. The room itself is fabulous, all glitter and sparkle and shiny metal, and the small-scale serving areas do a great job of providing personalized service; much of the food is cooked to your own order, the rest stands for a few minutes at most. The wide spectrum of offerings includes sushi, stir-fries, dim sum dumplings, barbecue, rotisserie chicken, and a carvery, plus ice cream and individually prepared salads; dinner sees extra seafood and meat dishes.

Le Village Buffet

Paris, 3655 Las Vegas Blvd S
☎702-946-7000. Breakfast $13, lunch $18, dinner $25. Eschewing the current vogue for incorporating every conceivable cuisine, Paris's buffet opts instead for including

▲ TANGERINE

only French dishes, and does so extremely well. The seafood is superb, whether it's the scallops, shrimp and crab in Sunday's brunch, or the Dover sole and rich *bouillabaisse* midweek; roast chicken comes fricasseed, as *coq au vin*, or with mustard; vegetables such as baby squash and pinto beans are super-fresh; and there's even a full French cheese board. At busy times, the seating is a little cramped, with the tables squeezed almost like an afterthought into the central square – a very Disney-esque French village – but the food is undeniably *magnifique*.

Todai Seafood Buffet

Desert Passage, Aladdin, 3663 Las Vegas Blvd S ☎702/892-0021. Lunch Mon–Fri $15, Sat & Sun $17; dinner Mon–Thurs $26, Fri–Sun $28. One of the very few Las Vegas buffets that's run as a standalone restaurant rather than a casino offshoot – and thus not to be confused with the Aladdin's own good-value *Spice Market* buffet – *Todai* belongs to a Californian chain specializing in magnificent all-you-can-eat Japanese spreads. It's seafood heaven, with unlimited sushi and sashimi plus salads, hot entrees, *ramen* and *udon* noodles, and both barbecued and teriyaki meats.

Bars and lounges

Caramel

Bellagio, 3600 Las Vegas Blvd S ☎702/693-8300, ⊛www.caramelbar .com. Daily 5pm–4am. An exclusive, expensive, and formal bar in the heart of Bellagio; perhaps a little too small to count as an ultra-lounge, but its opulent couches, marble tables, and pricey martinis offer a hip version of the high-roller lifestyle.

Cleopatra's Barge

Caesars Palace, 3500 Las Vegas Blvd S ☎702/731-7110. Daily 8.30pm–3am. Proving that there's still a place for campy kitsch in modern Las Vegas, this replica Egyptian ship, fronted by a golden figurehead and genuinely afloat in its own little moat at the front of the Appian Way shops, makes a fun stop-off on a night's bar-hopping.

Tangerine

TI, 3300 Las Vegas Blvd S ☎702/212-8140. Tues–Sat 5pm–4am; deck opens 3.30pm. Cover men $20, women $10. TI's new "speakeasy" changes character several times over the course of each day. When it opens in daylight, it offers fruit cocktails and Caribbean drumming; later its open-air deck serves as a crowded viewing station for the adjacent *Sirens of TI* show; and from 10.45pm onwards, an indoor stage hosts fifteen-minute burlesque performances every hour. There's also live and DJ music nightly.

Clubs and music venues

Krave

3663 Las Vegas Blvd S ☎702/836-0830, ⓦwww.kravelasvegas.com. Fri–Sun 10pm–6am. While the Strip doesn't yet hold a gay club as such, this self-styled "omni-sexual" club – located alongside Aladdin's Desert Passage mall – goes a long way towards filling the gap. Apart from the occasional women-only event, gay-friendly straights are welcome on nights geared primarily towards gay men and lesbians. On Friday and Saturday at 8pm, the club hosts *The Fashionistas*, an erotic fetish revue.

Light

Bellagio, 3600 Las Vegas Blvd S ☎702/693-8300. Thurs–Sun 10.30pm–4am. Cover $25. As you'd expect in Bellagio, *Light* is a classy, old-style nightclub, with paneled booths and table seating, for which reservations are essential. The music seems rather secondary, and varies at regular intervals to ensure all tastes are catered for.

Risqué

Paris, 3655 Las Vegas Blvd S ☎702/946-4589, ⓦwww.risquelv .com. Thurs–Sun 10pm–4am. Cover $20. Half bar, half nightclub, *Risqué* plays on its Paris location with plush European sofas and furnishings, and burlesque performances on Sundays. It also has a busy little dance floor, and, best of all, a handful of private open-air balconies above the Strip.

Vivid

The Venetian, 3265 Las Vegas Blvd S ☎702/414-4870. Wed–Sun 10.30pm–4am. Cover $20, $10 locals and hotel guests. Although operated by a major adult-film studio, and widely seen as the harbinger of an increasing presence for porn on the Strip, this small but much-hyped club stays firmly within Las Vegas's decency laws. Located on the walkway that leads into the Venetian from the bridge to TI, it's a plush, expensive lounge that features holographic dancing girls as well as live go-go dancers, and offers a cramped dance floor dominated by a wall of tiny lights.

Shows

Blue Man Group

The Venetian, 3265 Las Vegas Blvd S ⓦwww.venetian.com. In 2000, the Blue Man Group established themselves on the Strip where so many other shows – shows with stars, plots, and even words – have failed. And how have they done it? By the synchronized eating of breakfast cereal; by performing live endoscopies on audience members; by catching marshmallows tossed across the stage in their mouths. In fact, although (very funny) deadpan humor is a major component – and there's little choice but to be deadpan when you're coated in blue Latex – two further elements keep the crowds happy. First is the exhilarating music, which besides pieces set to the Sex Pistols and Jefferson Airplane, also includes lots of meaty drumming on industrial tubing from the Men themselves; and second are some truly stunning special effects. It's not for everyone, but breathtaking novelty is a good part of what Las Vegas is all about, and the Blue Men represent a welcome change from the now veteran Cirque de Soleil.

▲ THE IMPROV

Celine Dion

The Colosseum, Caesars Palace, 3500 Las Vegas Blvd S ☎702/731-7865. Seasonal, Wed–Sun 8.30pm. $87.50–225. If you have to ask whether it's worth $225 to see Celine Dion, the best-selling female singer of all time, perform in a show designed by Cirque du Soleil stalwart Franco Dragone, at a purpose-built 4000-seat Roman Colosseum at Caesars Palace, then the answer is probably "no." If you're a fan this will be the night of your life, but even if you're not, the sheer spectacle of the thing will probably be enough to keep you fascinated for its full hundred-minute length. Celine unquestionably has the voice to fill this amazing theater, and everyone gets to see and hear her very clearly indeed. To her own material, she adds a medley of songs by Etta James, Peggy Lee, and Frank Sinatra, and even (somewhat disturbingly) recalls being a "little nappy-headed boy" in Stevie Wonder's *I Wish*. The Cirque touches don't gel that well – think bewildered bellboys, deadpan clowns, and lots of silly shuffly dancing – but the staging is downright

awesome, with the live action brilliantly complemented by back projection on the world's largest LED screen. Finally, after a pause in which Celine breathlessly confesses how overcome she is by the sheer emotion of the whole occasion, she sings *that* song, whereupon everyone else is overcome, too.

Danny Gans

The Mirage, 3400 Las Vegas Blvd S ☎702/791-7111, ⓦwww .dannygansshow.com. Tues–Thurs, Sat & Sun 8pm. $100. His name may mean little anywhere else, but Danny Gans is very much the top of the Las Vegas tree. He's the kind of impersonator who announces each new impression, just in case you don't get it, and who craves permission from the audience to do something "as himself" in order to sing cloying, sentimental pap. Gans is certainly an energetic performer, carrying the whole ninety minutes in front of a live seven-piece band, and he has a smattering of good jokes, but not all of his "thousand voices" are amazing or even distinguishable, and you can end up feeling as though you've watched a one-man karaoke show – which can rankle, given the $100 pricetag. In fairness, Gans's audiences seem to love him; no doubt it helps if you are at least are familiar with his

Elton John's The Red Piano

Celine Dion currently plays the Colosseum at Caesars around 120 nights per year. The other principal residency here belongs to **Elton John**, who's scheduled to perform around 25 nights per year until 2007. Sir Elton's show is a glossy, hits-packed career retrospective called *The Red Piano*, that's as full of self-conscious camp – due in large part to David LaChappelle's exuberantly tacky and over-the-top stage design – as Celine's is of forthright diva sincerity.

The Central Strip | PLACES

targets, who range from John Cougar Mellencamp, Billy Joel, and Johnny Mathis to Macy Gray and Stevie Wonder, with the occasional oddball duet (Kermit the Frog and Jimmy Stewart, for example) thrown in.

The Improv

Harrah's, 3475 Las Vegas Blvd S ☎702/369-5111. Daily except Mon 8.30pm & 10.30pm. $27.50. Chicago's famous *Improv* has been at Harrah's since 1996, just up the stairs inside the main entrance. The formula remains the same, with three or four polished stand-ups per show rather than free-for-all improvisation. Big-name TV comedians make regular appearances here, so the standard of talent is dependably high.

Legends in Concert

The Imperial Palace, 3535 Las Vegas Blvd S ☎702/794-3261. Mon–Sat 7pm & 10pm. $40, including two drinks; ages 12 and under $25. The older of the Strip's two celebrity-tribute shows – the other, *American Superstars*, is at the Stratosphere – is also the better, with a changing roster of star impersonators ranging from Tina Turner to Rod Stewart. It's a quick-fire revue in which each cast member performs as just one star, with no lip-synching but plenty of showgirls in flamboyant costumes; by definition, there's little new about it, but it's good, undemanding fun. For musical prowess, the slick Four Tops are unbeatable, but the surreal re-creation of Michael Jackson's *Thriller*, with decaying corpses and dancing skeletons, is a joy to behold, and a tongue-in-cheek Elvis clowning through *Viva Las Vegas* makes a fitting finale. Even full-price tickets are

▼ LEGENDS IN CONCERT

reasonable value, but before you buy, check first whether they're giving them away on the sidewalk outside.

Mac King

Harrah's, 3475 Las Vegas Blvd S ⌖702/369-5111. Tues–Sat 1 & 3pm. $18.65. With tickets still priced at under $20, magician Mac King's afternoon show represents one of Las Vegas's best entertainment bargains. Hailing, like Lance Burton, from Kentucky (he even has a sponsorship deal with KFC), Mac's an endearingly wide-eyed innocent in a plaid suit who specializes in good old close-up magic, using ropes, cards, torn-up $20 bills and the like. His corny patter leaves plenty of room for good-natured improvised gags at the expense of those unwary audience members he lures up on stage.

Mystère

TI, 3300 Las Vegas Blvd S ⌖702/796-9999 or 800/963-9634, ⓦwww .cirquedusoleil.com. Wed–Sat 7.30pm & 10.30pm, Sun 4.30pm & 7.30pm. $95. When they first signed a ten-year contract with Treasure Island in 1993, Canada's Cirque du Soleil were widely seen as being too "way-out" for Las Vegas. In fact, *Mystère* proved to be the perfect postmodern product for the Strip; its success redefined the city's approach to entertainment, and made Cirque the Las Vegas standard, instead of the exception. Almost wordless, *Mystère* is all things to all people, ensuring audience involvement with a clever pre-show and further participation throughout. At base it's a showcase of fabulous circus skills, with tumblers, acrobats, trapeze artists, pole climbers, clowns, and a couple of amazing strong men. Unless you read the program, you might not even

▲ MYSTÈRE

realize there's a plot – something about two hungry babies of different species at opposite ends of the universe. However, whether you see its dreamscape symbolism as profound or vacuous, *Mystère* is such a visual feast – from the gloriously colorful costumes and fantastic animals to the fleeting glimpse of a devil-like creature stalking beneath the stage – with so much more going on than you could ever hope to follow, that it barely matters.

O

Bellagio, 3600 Las Vegas Blvd S ⌖702/796-9999 or 800/963-9634, ⓦwww.cirquedusoleil.com. Wed–Sun 7.30pm & 10.30pm. $99–150. Though in terms of sheer expense and extravagance this Cirque du Soleil extravaganza has now been upstaged by the company's even more ambitious *Kà* at the MGM Grand, it remains a remarkable testament to what can be done when cost is barely an issue. The name *O* is a pun on the French for "water," and any part of the stage in this purpose-built theater can at any time be submerged to any depth; one moment a performer may walk across a particular spot, the next someone may dive headfirst into that same spot from the high wire. With even less of a plot than *Mystère*, *O* is never portentous; from its beaming synchronized swimmers onwards, the cast simply revel in the opportunity to display their magnificent skills to maximum advantage. Highlights include a colossal trapeze frame draped like a pirate ship and crewed by a fearless assortment of acrobats and divers, and footmen flying through the air in swirls of velvet drapery.

Phantom of the Opera

The Venetian, 3265 Las Vegas Blvd S ☏877/883-6423, ⊛www.venetian .com. In its most serious bid yet to showcase big-ticket entertainment, the Venetian spent about $30 million building an 1800-seat theater to house this 90-minute, no-intermission version of Andrew Lloyd Webber's warhorse of a musical, *Phantom of the Opera*, set to open in the spring of 2006. Producers hoped to offset any die-hard fans' complaints about the shortened running time by having Webber and the original director, Harold Prince, oversee the production, and lavishing millions on the set – which will supposedly make the Broadway show look positively cheap by comparison.

The Second City

The Flamingo, 3555 Las Vegas Blvd S ☏702/733-3333. Tues–Thurs 8pm, Fri–Mon 8pm & 10:30pm. $35. Another Chicago import, this intimate little club features five seasoned performers in an often very funny revue that mixes scripted skits from the Second City repertoire with a fair amount of off-the-cuff improvisation. On Wednesdays at 8pm only, they go completely "scriptless" for audience-prompted improv.

V – The Ultimate Variety Show

V Theater, Desert Passage, Aladdin, 3667 Las Vegas Blvd S ☏702/932-1818, ⊛www.vtheshow.com. Daily 7pm & 9pm. $59–69, under-13s half price. This old-fashioned but enjoyable revue show gives half a dozen variety acts – who tend to be comedians, jugglers, strong men and the like, rather than singers – around ten minutes each to prove their worth. Seating is unreserved, so arrive early to get a decent view. If the hilarious Russ Merlin is on the bill, be sure not to miss it.

Shops

Appian Way

Caesars Palace, 3500 Las Vegas Blvd S ☏702/731-7222. Individual store hours vary. It's the Forum shops that garner most of the attention at Caesars Palace, but don't neglect the *other* mall here, the Appian Way, which has occupied a couple of hallways behind the lobby and central casino area since 1978. Its upscale stores – including Cartier jewelers and the Italian clothing specialist Bernini Couture – radiate out from a domed area that holds an 18-foot marble replica of Michaelangelo's *David*, identical to the original in every respect except for remaining uncircumcised.

Desert Passage

The Aladdin, 3663 Las Vegas Blvd S ☏888/800-8284, ⊛www .desertpassage.com. Mon–Thurs & Sun

10am–11pm, Fri & Sat 10am–midnight. Although the Desert Passage mall rivals the Forum and the Grand Canal in both scale and the range of its stores, it has so far failed to attract the same volume of customers as either. That may change when the adjoining Aladdin becomes Planet Hollywood; expect the Middle Eastern theming to be replaced with something even more spectacular, but most of the businesses to remain in place. The stores here are geared a little less exclusively towards tourists than in most hotel malls (which could help explain the lack of traffic), with the large Z Gallerie among the best home furnishings stores in the city. Nonetheless, the Desert Passage holds dozens of appealing fashion and specialty outlets, including Betsey Johnson, French Connection, Hilo Hattie, Napoleon, Victoria's Secret, and The Sharper Image, as well as a roster of excellent restaurants, headed by *Commander's Palace*.

The Forum

Caesars Palace, 3500 Las Vegas Blvd S ☎702/893-4800, ⓦwww.forumshops .com. Mon–Thurs & Sun 10am–11pm, Fri & Sat 10am–midnight. The mall that kick-started Las Vegas's shopping boom in 1992 continues to be the most successful in the United States, generating seven times as much income per square foot as the national average. Having doubled in size in 1997, the Forum added as much space again in 2002, and then expanded two years later onto a second level, reached by a breathtaking spiral escalator. While the shopping is quite good, the Forum's success is largely due to it being a great tourist destination in its own right. The basic concept is

▲ GRAND CANAL SHOPPES

irresistible, with faux-Roman columns and fountains everywhere, "statues" that come alive, and an artificial sky that wheels each hour between dawn and dusk. Among the hundred-plus stores, clothing choices range from Gap and Banana Republic, through Diesel, Ted Baker, and DKNY, to Emporio Armani and Gianni Versace; there are ten jewelers and thirteen shoe stores, including Footworks and a showpiece Nike Town; and specialty outlets include the excellent Virgin Megastore, the Strip's best option for buying CDs or DVDs. The Forum doesn't have a food court as such – there's one not far away in the casino proper – but it does hold some fine restaurants, such as *Chinois*, *Stage Deli*, and *The Palm*.

The Grand Canal Shoppes

The Venetian, 3355 Las Vegas Blvd S ☎702/414-4500, ⓦwww .grandcanalshoppes.com. Sun–Thurs 10am–11pm, Fri & Sat 10am–midnight. Naturally enough, the shopping mall at the Venetian claims to draw its inspiration from Venice itself, but its true model is rather closer to hand. From its false Italian sky (here set permanently to early evening) down to many of the actual stores, the Grand Canal Shoppes slavishly imitates the most effective elements of the Forum across the street, and in some respects actually surpasses it. The Grand Canal itself is breathtaking, not least for the sheer chutzpah of locating a full-blown waterway (complete with working gondolas) on the second story of the building, while with its "open-air" restaurants, St Mark's Square really does feel like a vibrant city square. In terms of pure shopping, however, it's not quite large or varied enough to outdo the Forum, though the Shoppes are easier to reach, either via escalators immediately inside the main casino entrance, or a moving walkway from the Strip. Both entryways lead to an impressive anteroom decorated with dramatic frescoes, beyond which you'll find a number

of conventional mall outlets. Further in, the general emphasis is more consistently upscale than at the Forum, with designer clothing stores like Gandini and Pal Zileri, and jewelry specialists such as Ca' D'Oro (gold), Erwin Pearl (pearls), and Simayof (diamonds). Less familiar "shoppes" include some making their first appearance outside Venice, like Il Prato, selling carnival masks and paper goods, and Ripa de Monti, which specializes in exquisite glassware.

Via Bellagio

Bellagio, 3600 Las Vegas Blvd S ☏702/693-7111. Daily 10am–midnight. While Via Bellagio isn't nearly as large as the Forum, Grand Canal Shoppes, or Desert Passage, its single-minded focus on the very top end of the spectrum has made it the chicest place to shop in Las Vegas. Even so, its stores still epitomize the city's democratic approach to shopping: when even the most scruffily dressed customer may turn out to be a big spender, anyone is welcome to browse. Just ten stores are ranged on either side of this plushly carpeted walkway that connects the north end of Bellagio (facing Caesars) with the Strip. As well as Gucci, Georgio Armani, Chanel, Dior, Tiffany & Co, and Hermès, the catch-all Bellagio Collections store stocks clothing, footwear, and accessories by more than a dozen other internationally known designers.

▲ VIA BELLAGIO

The North Strip

Before the advent of the showcase Wynn Las Vegas in 2005, the northern end of the Strip had witnessed far less recent development than the areas further south. Although big names from the past survived, several casinos here had come to be seen as embarrassing poor relations in the new Las Vegas. Even the Monorail bypasses the North Strip altogether. Things may be about to change, however. The Fashion Show Mall has already dramatically upgraded itself, while Wynn seems set to revitalize the neighborhood. If so, the Stardust, Riviera, and New Frontier are all likely to be replaced by modern super-resorts, while another may well soon occupy the former site of the Wet'n'Wild water park, alongside the Sahara.

Wynn Las Vegas

3131 Las Vegas Blvd S ☎ 866/770-7108, ⓦ www.wynnlasvegas.com. Las Vegas's newest mega–casino dominates the north part of the Strip, standing just north of the Venetian and across from the Fashion Show Mall. Wynn Las Vegas is the latest project of entrepreneur *extraordinaire* Steve Wynn, previously responsible for the Mirage and Bellagio. He bought the veteran Desert Inn in April 2000, using $275 million gained from his sale of the Mirage organization to MGM. That gave him a large chunk of prime Vegas property, twice the size of the Mirage and TI combined, on which he originally planned to build a casino resort called Le Rêve (French for "The Dream"), named for his favorite of the Picassos in his personal collection. The bankers who had to stump up the rest of the $2.7 billion Wynn needed, however, felt this was a little too abstract, and so the project took on his name (with its obvious gambler-friendly connotations) instead.

As Wynn Las Vegas did not open until April 2005 – after this book went to press – you'll have to judge for yourself whether that $2.7 billion was

▼ WYNN LAS VEGAS

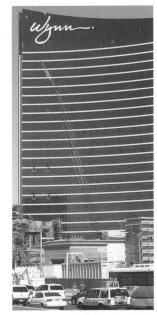

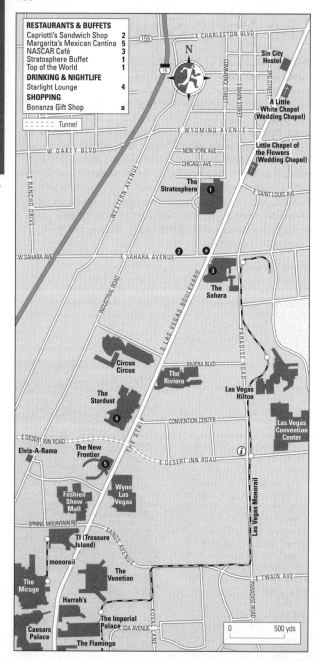

RESTAURANTS & BUFFETS
Capriotti's Sandwich Shop   **2**
Margarita's Mexican Cantina   **5**
NASCAR Café   **3**
Stratosphere Buffet   **1**
Top of the World   **1**
DRINKING & NIGHTLIFE
Starlight Lounge   **4**
SHOPPING
Bonanza Gift Shop   **a**
------ Tunnel

spent wisely. Wynn dropped hints in advance about the new resort being "water-themed," and commented that, unlike Bellagio, the Mirage, and TI – which he said were "pictures to be viewed from outside" – this one was designed from the inside out.

Aimed at the very top end of the market, Wynn Las Vegas was scheduled to offer 18 restaurants, an 18-hole golf course, a spa, Wynn's personal art collection, a parade of 29 exclusive shops (Chanel, Dior, Jean Paul Gaultier, Manolo Blahnik, and the like), and a car dealership (the first on the Strip) selling only Ferraris and Maseratis. Unlike other high-end casinos whose celebrity chefs split their time between Vegas and their home cities, its restaurants are run by lesser-known but respected chefs whom Wynn convinced to move here. The exception is Daniel Boulud, who's opening a Vegas branch of New York's celebrated *Daniel*, serving pricey gourmet contemporary French cuisine.

The entertainment on hand is similarly top-notch, with at least two long-running shows, including a new production by Cirque de Soleil pioneer Franco Dragone called *Le Rêve*, and the edgy Tony-winning musical *Avenue Q* in its first non-Broadway engagement – both in their own purpose-built theaters.

The sleek, black, 50-story building holds 2700 hotel rooms, and is shielded from the noise and tumult of the Strip behind an artificial mountain with its own cascading waterfall. Although a massive space (5.6 million square feet), Wynn Las Vegas is intended to seem more intimate, with restaurants concealed from the racket of the gambling floor. The casino itself has all the usual features, plus at least one that's unique: each chip used there contains an RFID (radio frequency identification device), allowing management to track its location and weed out fakes used by scammers.

Elvis-A-Rama

3401 Industrial Rd ☎702/309-7200, ⊛www.elvisarama.com. Daily 10am–6pm. $10, or $22 including show. Located between the Fashion Show Mall and the I-15 interstate, but too far from the Strip for walking to be advisable (free shuttle buses pick up from any Strip hotel), the Elvis-A-Rama museum contains just enough Presley memorabilia to satisfy avid fans. Personal possessions of the King – like the 1955 concert limo he bought with his $5000 RCA signing bonus – are complemented by stage costumes, movie posters, and mass-produced souvenirs such as lipsticks, keyrings, and bubble-gum cards. If all this stokes your fancy for something to take home, a gift store fortunately sells contemporary Elvis tat. While it can't match the Liberace Museum in terms of scale, obsessiveness, or intimate personal connection, Elvis-A-Rama does at least offer live impersonator shows on its small stage at 2pm and 4pm daily.

The New Frontier

3120 Las Vegas Blvd S ☎800/421-7806, ⊛www.frontierlv.com. The New Frontier is the oldest casino still surviving on the Strip. Originally named the Last Frontier, it started out in 1942 as a glorified hundred-room motel that milked its desert setting for every drop of Old West appeal. Combining crude

▲ GUARDIAN ANGEL CATHEDRAL

log-cabin trimmings with glittering neon, it was marketed as "the Early West in Modern Splendor."

For a long time, the casino was under the influence of the Mob, who remained in covert control for several years even after Howard Hughes acquired the rebuilt and renamed hotel in 1967. Hughes was living across the Strip in the Desert Inn at the time (see box below), and is said to have bought the New Frontier because he was alarmed that its new sign (at 184ft the tallest in the world) might blow down and hit his home. That same worrisome sign is still standing, looking deeply old-fashioned with its tame slogan: "choice beef, poultry and seafood at affordable prices."

Current New Frontier owner Phil Ruffin has repeatedly declared his intention to implode the entire property and replace it with a billion-dollar mega-casino. As of early 2005, plans remained vague, though Ruffin did announce at one point that the new casino would be San Francisco–themed. The opening of Wynn Las Vegas may finally make this dream a reality, but for the moment all that's certain is that Ruffin and legendary entrepreneur Donald Trump are building two predominantly residential "Trump Towers" behind the New Frontier.

For the moment, the New Frontier is the last Strip property where it's still possible to park your car in the front lot, while the casino itself – sorry, "Gambling Hall" – remains locked in the Wild West tradition. A chuck wagon waits outside for its owner to return,

Howard Hughes in Las Vegas

By welcoming Howard Hughes as a guest at Thanksgiving in 1966, the now-defunct Desert Inn inadvertently spearheaded Las Vegas's move toward corporate domination. As New Year approached, the management insisted that the non-gambling Hughes check out before the annual influx of high-roll gamblers arrived. Hughes instead took over the whole hotel, buying its license to operate until 2002 (although not the casino itself) for $13.2 million.

Hughes remained at the Desert Inn for four years, living on the ninth floor with curtains drawn and windows taped over, and keeping the entire eighth floor empty. During that time, he bought enough casinos to become Nevada's largest single operator, despite seldom, if never, allowing even his closest associates to see him. Tales of his eccentricity abound; quite apart from storing all his urine in jars in his closet, and having total transfusions of Mormon blood, he canceled the hotel's traditional Easter Egg hunt because he loathed children.

while a vintage slot machine in the shape of John Wayne stands immediately inside the saloon-style doors.

Guardian Angel Cathedral

302 Cathedral Way ☎702/735-5241. Sunday mass at 8am, 9.30am, 11am, 12.30pm & 5pm. Open to visitors Mon–Fri 7.30am–3.30pm, Sat 10am–6.30pm, Sun 7.30am–1.30pm & 4–6pm. Though dwarfed to the point of invisibility by the surrounding cathedrals to Mammon, the starkly angular Guardian Angel Cathedral, just north of Wynn Las Vegas and one of the Strip's least likely sights, is a genuine Roman Catholic cathedral. Looking much newer than its construction date of 1963 would suggest, Guardian Angel is a welcome haven from the frenzy outside its doors, but it does feature some true Las Vegas touches. The baptismal font resembles an over-sized marble jacuzzi, coin-in-the-slot electric "candles" line the aisles, and of course there's a gift store. Best of all is the stained-glass window depicting the Stardust, the Sands, and the Hilton rising above a maze of concrete freeways.

The Stardust

3000 Las Vegas Blvd S ☎866/642-3120, ⓦwww.stardustlv.com. Though long since over-shadowed by nouveau-riche newcomers, the Stardust can look back on a career as a major Las Vegas player. A glittering child of the space age, it burst on the scene in 1958 as the world's largest hotel, no more than two stories high, perhaps, but cascading neon from its eye-catching, Sputnik-inspired Strip facade.

All that dazzling starlight served to conceal some murky figures lurking in the back-ground. The Stardust's true owner was actually Chicago mobster Sam Giancana, with control passing during the 1970s to a loose consortium of Mid-western Mafia families. Martin Scorsese's 1995 movie *Casino* tells the story of the ensuing scandals and bloodshed in enter-taining detail, while *Showgirls* commemorates the fact that for 33 years, the Stardust hosted the French nude revue *Lido de Paris*.

The Stardust is these days rather more staid, with the Wayner himself making all-too-regular appearances at his namesake Wayne Newton Theater, and the main appeal for visitors resting in its very large, sophisticated Race and Sports Book. Its current owners, the Boyd Corporation, reportedly want to tear the place down altogether and replace it with a billion-dollar, three-thousand-room resort called Borgata West, hoping to imitate the runaway success they've had with the Atlantic City Borgata. As with the New Frontier, success for Wynn Las Vegas will probably spell doom for the Stardust.

▲ THE STARDUST

PLACES   **The North Strip**

▲ THE RIVIERA

The Riviera

2901 Las Vegas Blvd S ☎ 800/634-6753, 🌐 www.theriviera.com. In 1955, the new Riviera held considerable novelty value. Merely by remaining erect, it confounded skeptics who predicted that the sands of Las Vegas could never bear the weight of its unbelievable nine stories, while its style, modeled on the French Côte d'Azur, seemed both exotic and romantic.

Today, with any pretense at creating a Mediterranean ambience long since abandoned, the Riviera boasts an exuberantly garish facade, with neon stars, stripes, and curlicues swirling across a towering curved mirror. After that, the mundane casino inside – which holds a separate arcade known as Nickel Town, devoted exclusively to nickel slots and cheap snacks – comes as a disappointment. However, the Riviera does at least still have four showrooms in operation, continuing to entice gamblers with traditional semi-sexy entertainment. Much like its neighbors, the Riviera is currently surrounded by rumors that it may soon be demolished to make room for something more in keeping with modern Las Vegas.

Circus Circus

2880 Las Vegas Blvd S ☎ 877/224-7287, 🌐 www.circuscircus.com. A rare constant in the ever-changing world of Las Vegas, Circus Circus has remained true to itself ever since opening back in 1969. Back in the 1960s, combining children's entertainment with casino gambling under a single roof was a radical concept. Later on, that idea was embraced as a surefire money-spinning formula. Now it's a discredited cliché; and yet Circus Circus carries on regardless.

Circus Circus began life as Jay Sarno's follow-up to his mega-hit Caesars Palace, designed to appeal to fun-seeking families and high rollers alike. The basic theme, of a hectic, spit-and-sawdust gaming area overlooked by a carnival-style "midway," featuring sideshows and circus performers, was much as it remains today. It took a while to get the details right, however. Not only did the original Circus Circus lack hotel accommodation, but it even charged admission. On top of that, the midway was at first a sleazy affair, including attractions like the "Bed Toss" sideshow, which invited patrons to throw softballs to spill naked showgirls out of satin beds. Only after Sarno sold his stake in 1974 did the place turn both wholesome and profitable, so much so that

Fear and Loathing

In one of the more memorable passages from the late Hunter S. Thompson's *Fear and Loathing in Las Vegas*, he writes, "Circus Circus is what the whole hep world would be doing on Saturday night if the Nazis had won the war."

▲ MIDWAY, CIRCUS CIRCUS

Circus Circus Enterprises (later the Mandalay Resort Group) went on to become the leading casino operator in the country.

Though the main Circus Circus building is low-rise by Las Vegas standards, its presence on the Strip is unmistakable, thanks to the gigantic Lucky-the-Clown neon sign and marquee-like canopy. Clowns, contortionists, and trapeze artists still cavort on **The Midway** stage upstairs between 11am and midnight daily, surrounded by fairground stalls and attractions. Behind it, the whole complex stretches so far back that there's an in-house monorail link to help exhausted guests return to their rooms.

No one could mistake Circus Circus for a sophisticated joint as there's nothing glamorous about its three low-stakes, high-volume casinos, while the low ceilings make this one of the most claustrophobic and smoky places to gamble in town.

The main feature of Circus Circus that lures in tourists with children is the five-acre **Adventuredome** theme park (Mon–Thurs 11am–6pm, Fri & Sat 10am–midnight, Sun 10am–8pm; ⓦwww.adventuredome.com; $4–6 individual attractions, $22 all-day wristband, $14 kids under 4ft), sheltered beneath a huge bubble of pink glass at the back of the property. Entered only through the casino proper, the dome encloses a Disneyland-esque melange of rides and sideshows. Its central feature is a big red-rock mountain holding the corkscrewing Canyon Blaster roller coaster (rated by aficionados as the best in town), the spinning Chaos ride, and the Rim Runner water chute, which passes such dioramas as an Indian pueblo village and a herd of animatronic dinosaurs.

The Sahara

2535 Las Vegas Blvd S ⓣ888/696-2121, ⓦwww.saharavegas.com. The Sahara looks set to be the last bastion of a once-ubiquitous Las Vegas tradition. Strip casinos used to relish the city's desert setting, but with the demise

▼ CIRCUS CIRCUS

▲ THE SAHARA

of soul mates like the Dunes and the Sands, and the Aladdin going Hollywood, only the Sahara (which first appeared in 1952) still caters to those who nurture *Arabian Nights* fantasies of sheiks at play in the shifting sands. Sadly, though, the trademark camels that formerly stood above the main entrance have been put out to pasture, in favor of a glittering golden dome encircled by Moorish arches.

The Sahara also has a long-standing association with cars, a passion that dates back to the 1960s, when Las Vegas was the auto-racing capital of the West, as celebrated in the movie *Viva Las Vegas*. Indeed, Elvis Presley and his entourage made the Sahara their home during the shooting. Today, the quite prominent *NASCAR Café* straddles the entrance to the indoor **Cyber Speedway** (Sun–Thurs 10am–10pm, Fri & Sat 10am–11pm; $10 per ride), where each participant faces a private screen and "drives" a three-quarter-size Indy car that bucks and surges in response to the slightest touch of the controls. At any one time, eight cars race each other around video renditions of either the Indianapolis racetrack or the streets of Las Vegas; printouts at the end reveal which driver

beat the rest. The more you do it, the more likely you are to win, so the whole experience is fiendishly addictive. Alternatively, you can pay $5 for the much less heart-thumping experience of watching a 3-D movie of the real thing.

The Sahara's conspicuous **Speed Ride** (Sun–Thurs 10am–10pm, Fri & Sat 10am–midnight; $10 per ride, or $20 for all-day pass) is a "magnetic-induction ride" – a roller coaster, to you or me – in which the cars crash through the outer wall of the *NASCAR Café*, loop through the open air above the Strip, and then climb a 250-foot tower. The thrill is real enough, but at $10 for 48 seconds, it's all over a bit too fast.

The Stratosphere

2000 Las Vegas Blvd S ☎888/236-7495, ⊛www.stratlv.com. For many years, the unsavory stretch of Las Vegas Boulevard north of Sahara Avenue was not regarded as really belonging to the Strip – not least because it lies within the city limits of Las Vegas rather than Clark County. These days, however, it's dominated by the mighty Stratosphere Tower, which serves as a symbolic northern border to the great neon way, a taller but somehow less impressive counterpart to the Strip's southern outpost, Mandalay Bay.

In 1979, one of the great Las Vegas hucksters, Bob Stupak, opened the immensely tacky Vegas World casino here, half a dozen blocks up from the Sahara, and immediately began talking about building the world's tallest tower alongside it. Problems with financing and construction meant that by the time the Stratosphere was eventually completed in 1996, it ended up being simply the tallest building west of the Mississippi, while panicking investors forced Stupak to replace Vegas World itself with a higher-class hotel. Initially a financial disaster, in the longer run it has done surprisingly well, kept busy particularly by European tour groups.

At ground level, the Stratosphere is far from enthralling. For sightseers, the only reason to come is the 1149-foot Tower itself. It's hardly a great piece of architecture, but the multi-colored flashes and spirals of light around its base provide one of Las Vegas's finest displays of neon, while the "pod" at the summit fully lives up to expectations.

Tickets to reach the top are sold up on the second floor, while the elevators themselves start at the far end of a shopping-and-souvenir mall (Sun–Thurs 10am–midnight, Fri & Sat 10am–2am; $9, discounts for guests). After a 75-second ascent, you emerge outdoors, on the 109th floor, to be confronted by an astounding 360° panorama of the city. The views are even better from the floor below, where the windows of the indoor gallery angle out over the edge, and captions explain every detail on view.

Despite the lack of the much touted and never constructed Belly of the Beast ride – in which a King Kong–shaped elevator would carry passengers up the outside of the tower, and then, under airplane attack, let them go – the uppermost

▼ THE STRATOSPHERE

level of the Stratosphere does offer three rather wonderfully demented **thrill rides** (Sun–Thurs 10am–midnight, Fri & Sat 10am–2am. Rides individually priced; combinations range up to the $25 all-day Unlimited Package). The High Roller ($4), the world's highest roller coaster, rumbles around the outside; X-Scream ($8) dangles passengers over the edge in a precarious gondola; and the ludicrous but terrifying Big Shot ($8) is an open-air couch that shunts to the top of an additional 160-foot spire, then free-falls down again.

Restaurants

Capriotti's Sandwich Shop

322 W Sahara Ave ☎702/474-0229, ⓦwww.capriottis.com. Lunch only, closed Sun. For a lunchtime bargain, it's worth straying a short distance west of the Strip to this outlet of the popular chain – one of many in the city – which is renowned for its enormous $6–10 deli subs and sandwiches, prepared using fresh ingredients, like turkey roasted on the premises.

Margarita's Mexican Cantina

The New Frontier, 3120 Las Vegas Blvd S ☎702/794-8433. This appealingly old-fashioned bar-cum-restaurant on the New Frontier's main casino floor – where the south-of-the-border decor includes murals, fake vine trellises, and high-backed wooden chairs – offers the best-value Mexican food on the Strip. Warm tortillas and dips are served as soon as you sit down, while the satisfyingly substantial tacos, burritos, or fajitas cost $8–12, a "feast platter" for two is $23, and you can pick up a

margarita to wash it all down for just $2.

NASCAR Café

The Sahara, 2535 Las Vegas Blvd S ☎702/737-2875, ⓦwww .nascarcafelasvegas.com. If you find yourself in the car-mad Sahara at all, you're probably here for the NASCAR connection, so this garish sports-themed eatery will be right up your street. Always packed with enthusiastic race fans admiring the memorabilia (especially the centerpiece 34-foot "Carzilla," the world's largest stock car), it serves a predictable menu of burgers and barbecue sandwiches for $7–10, plus pizza, pasta, steak, and ribs for a little more.

Top of the World

The Stratosphere, 2000 Las Vegas Blvd S ☎702/380-7711. So long as you're happy to settle for good rather than gourmet food, dining at this 106th-floor revolving restaurant is an utterly memorable experience; the view is simply phenomenal. The best time to come is after dark, when the menu – a catch-all mixture of Californian, quasi-Asian, and routine American dishes – is more interesting than at lunch, and the lights of the Strip are at their most spectacular. Typical dinner entrees, such as Santa Fe rotisserie chicken or prime rib, cost $25–32; be sure to order the miniature chocolate Stratosphere Tower for dessert ($10).

Buffets

Stratosphere Buffet

The Stratosphere, 2000 Las Vegas Blvd S ☎702/380-7777. Breakfast $7.25, lunch $9, dinner Mon–Thurs & Sat $12, Fri & Sun $15. Like much else in the Stratosphere, the

Buffet is rather half-hearted in its themed decoration (consisting of little more than a half-dozen little hot-air balloons) and its ambience (or lack thereof, being basically a passageway on the north side of the building) but it does offer pretty good value, nonetheless. The food is reasonable without being exceptional, and with Mexican, Chinese, and Italian offerings as well as the predictable American, it should satisfy most appetites. Note that visiting the top of the Tower entitles you to a discount here. The premium rates on Fridays and Saturdays reflect an extra leavening of seafood.

Bars and lounges

Starlight Lounge

The Stardust, 3000 Las Vegas Blvd S ☎702/732-6111. Daily 24hr. While it's probably not worth going far out of your way to see it, if you're in the area, stop by the Stardust's lounge bar, a true vintage throwback to old-style Las Vegas, complete with plush armchairs.

The Shows

Amazing Johnathan

The Riviera, 2901 Las Vegas Blvd S ☎702/794-9433, ⊛www.amazingj .com. Daily except Thurs 10pm. $47–58. Stressing the Amazing Johnathan's unbridled craziness, the advertising and pre-show build-up here might lead you to expect a crude late-night gross-out. In fact, barring the cartoonish violence he directs against his ditzy blonde assistant "Psychic Tanya," Johnathan's quite a lovable character. He's basically a comedy magician, with the emphasis on the comedy, meaning that he barely completes a trick all evening. That's probably for the best, anyway, as carefully honed patter and hilarious skits like "Bad Karate Theater" make this one of Las Vegas's funniest shows.

Avenue Q

Wynn Las Vegas, 3131 Las Vegas Blvd S ⊛www.avenueq.com. Although it hadn't opened at the time of writing, the production of *Avenue Q* at Wynn Las Vegas is expected to be almost exactly

▲ AVENUE Q

PLACES The North Strip

the same as the surprise Broadway hit that won the 2004 Tony for Best Musical. Given how off-center and suffused with Gen-X irony the story is – about a Brooklyn neighborhood populated by slackers, hilariously R-rated puppets (including one gay Republican) and Gary Coleman – this might seem an unlikely choice for Vegas audiences. But, then, the show wasn't expected to win the Tony or have one of the most popular recent runs on Broadway, either. It doesn't hurt that the songs (by a team that includes some *Sesame Street* veterans) are fantastic.

Crazy Girls

The Riviera, 2901 Las Vegas Blvd S ☎702/794-9433. Daily except Thurs 8pm. $42 & $53, including two drinks; no under-18s. The crowd at the Strip's best-known "adult revue" consists largely of overweight frat boys, interspersed with a few swinging middle-aged couples, crammed in at little tables and emitting the occasional frightened squeal when the dancers come too close. Urged on by a lackluster (female) comedian, eight world-weary and none-too-crazy showgirls, not only topless but also sexless for good measure, dance their desultory way through a set of hackneyed chestnuts.

Le Rêve

Wynn Las Vegas, 3131 Las Vegas Blvd S ⊛www.wynnlasvegas.com. Thurs–Mon 7.30 & 10.30pm. $110. Supposedly the first person whom Steve Wynn contacted when he got the idea for his new casino was former Cirque impresario Franco Dragone. *Le Rêve* is the result – an extravagently produced water-themed

show with a 70-person cast that focuses on acrobatic stunts and audience intimacy. None of the 2100-odd seats in the theater will be more than 42 feet from the action. Even though it wasn't open for review at the time of writing, given Dragone's track record and Wynn's deep pockets (production cost estimates top $100 million), it's safe to say that *Le Rêve* will at the very least give audiences their money's worth.

Shops

Bonanza Gift Shop

2460 Las Vegas Blvd S ☎702/385-7359. Daily 8am–midnight. Across from the Sahara and just south of the Stratosphere, the "World's Largest Gift Store" is really not all that big, but it's still the single best outlet for all those tacky souvenirs you'd hope to find in Las Vegas. Beyond the predictable array of *chotchkes* – used playing cards from all the casinos, gaming boards, fuzzy dice, whoopee cushions, fart candy, postcards, and nudie ballpoint pens – you'll find a more surreal world of Las Vegas snowglobes, Elvis clocks, and inflatable aliens.

The Fashion Show Mall

3200 Las Vegas Blvd S ☎702/369-0704, ⊛www.thefashionshow.com. Mon–Fri 10am–9pm, Sat 10am–8pm, Sun 11am–6pm. The Fashion Show Mall caused a sensation when it opened in 1981, being the first significant shopping mall to appear on the Strip. Twenty years on, however, it had become a seen-it-all-before snooze, hence the massive expansion and revitalization that was completed in 2003. Behind a new, glittering frontage, topped by the bizarre 300-foot disc-shaped "Cloud" (which sometimes resembles a high-fashion hat and sometimes a UFO), it now rivals any mall in the city. While not a must-see attraction like the Forum or Grand Canal Shoppes, the Fashion Show Mall does surpass them by offering full-sized department stores, including Las Vegas's first Nord-strom and Bloomingdale's, as well as

▲ FASHION SHOW MALL

Neiman Marcus, Saks Fifth Avenue, Macy's, Dillard's, and Robinsons-May. Smaller specialty outlets include the appealing Paul Frank's out front, Japanese kitsch purveyors Sanrio, and an Apple store. There's also a large fast-food court with a view of the Strip as well as several proper restaurants.

Wedding chapels

Little Chapel of the Flowers

1717 Las Vegas Blvd S ☎702/735-4331 or 800/843-2410, ⊛www .littlechapel.com. A rather twee, traditional establishment, with two antique-furnished chapels off the lobby, that's most notorious for being the site where Dennis Rodman and Carmen Electra were briefly hitched. Weddings range upwards from $195; for $1195 you get a helicopter ride to the Grand Canyon thrown in, while for $4995 you can be married on a yacht on Lake Mead.

A Little White Chapel

1301 Las Vegas Blvd S ☎702/382-5943 or 800/545-8111, ⊛www .alittlewhitechapel.com. Daily 24hr. The chapel (indeed, little and white) where Bruce Willis and Demi Moore married each other, and Michael Jordan and Joan Collins (whose names are on the sign out front) married other, non-famous people. More recently, in January 2004, it was the scene of Britney Spears' misconceived and ill-fated wedding to child-hood friend Jason Alexander. Open all day every day, with drive-thru ceremonies available in the roofed-over driveway (or "Tunnel of Love") for those in a major hurry.

Downtown Las Vegas

Downtown Las Vegas is not a "downtown" in the conventional sense, having never developed a significant infrastructure of stores and other businesses outside its dozen or so casinos. The city of Las Vegas promotes the area so heavily because, since the Strip is located in Clark County, the casinos here are the only ones in Las Vegas that pay city taxes. However, they remain poor relations to the Strip giants, taking in only about one-seventh as much gaming revenue. If you come to Las Vegas specifically to gamble, there's good reason to spend time downtown – the odds tend to be better, the rooms cheaper, and the atmosphere a bit more casual – but otherwise you miss little by avoiding it altogether.

The Fremont Street Experience

Fremont Street, between Main and 4th ⓦ www.vegasexperience.com. Nightly, hourly on the hour from sunset until midnight. Free. The gigantic metal mesh of the Fremont Street Experience stretches over Fremont for four entire blocks, the area once known as "Glitter Gulch." Ninety feet high, this so-called "Celestial Vault" shades the pedestrianized street during the day, but comes into its own at night, when twelve million LED modules turn it into a giant movie screen. There's no plot or content to the free hourly shows, just pure eye-catching spectacle and a blast of soft rock; spectators gather below to gasp, stagger, and applaud as they're catapulted into space, draped with US flags, or menaced by colossal swarming snakes.

Built in 1999, the Fremont Street Experience is sponsored by the downtown casinos, which cooperate by turning off their lights during each six-minute show. In 2003, a federal appeals court rejected the casinos' claim to "own" Fremont Street, ruling that they have no right to eject such "undesirables" as downtown's considerable homeless population from the district.

▲ FREMONT STREET EXPERIENCE

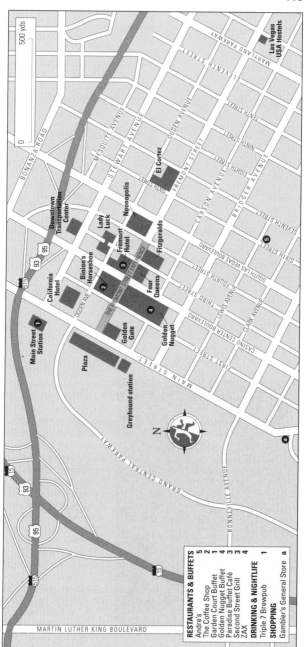

500 yds

0

BONANZA ROAD

Downtown Transportation Center

California Hotel

Main Street Station 1

Plaza

Greyhound station

Binion's Horseshoe

Golden Gate

Golden Nugget

Lady Luck

Neonopolis

Fremont Hotel

Four Queens

Fitzgeralds

El Cortez

MESQUITE AVENUE

STEWART AVENUE

OGDEN AVENUE

FREMONT STREET

THE FREMONT STREET EXPERIENCE

CARSON AVENUE

BRIDGER AVENUE

LEWIS AVENUE

CLARK AVENUE

CASINO CENTER BOULEVARD

BONNEVILLE AVENUE

GRAND CENTRAL PARKWAY

MARTIN LUTHER KING BOULEVARD

MARYLAND PARKWAY

ELEVENTH STREET

TENTH STREET

NINTH STREET

EIGHTH STREET

SIXTH STREET

SEVENTH STREET

FOURTH STREET

THIRD STREET

FIRST STREET

MAIN STREET

SOUTH LAS VEGAS BOULEVARD

Las Vegas USA Hostels

N

RESTAURANTS & BUFFETS
Andre's 5
The Coffee Shop 2
Garden Court Buffet 1
Golden Nugget Buffet 4
Paradise Buffet Café 3
Second Street Grill 3
ZAX 4
DRINKING & NIGHTLIFE
Triple 7 Brewpub 1
SHOPPING
Gambler's General Store a

The Golden Gate

1 E Fremont St ☎ 800/426-1906,
🌐 www.goldengatecasino.net.
Unique for Las Vegas in being
genuinely old, rather than
simply themed to look old, the
Golden Gate has stood at the
west end of Fremont Street
since 1906 (original phone
number: 1), when the city
itself was just a year old. Barely
changed since a third story was
added in 1931, its dark, wood-
paneled interior now feels tiny
and unexciting. Many Las Vegas
visitors, however, still make a
special pilgrimage to buy the
legendary 99¢ shrimp cocktails
it has been serving since 1959.

The Golden Nugget

129 E Fremont St ☎ 800/846-5336,
🌐 www.goldennugget.com. The
Golden Nugget is generally
described as being the one
downtown casino that matches
the extravagance and splendor
of the Strip. It doesn't. While
indeed a bright, glittery place
that attracts a more upmarket
clientele than any other downtown casino, it's nonetheless very
far from counting as a must-see
destination. The Golden Nugget
opened in 1946 and was originally designed to ape the look
of opulent nineteenth-century
San Francisco saloons. Several
decades later, it's best known
as the place where Las Vegas's
premier gaming entrepreneur,
Steve Wynn, gained his first
foothold in the casino business, during the 1970s, before
building the Mirage, Bellagio,
and Wynn on the Strip. MGM-
Mirage eventually sold the
Golden Nugget for $215 million
in 2004, evidence that the major
conglomerates were no longer
interested in the paltry profits to
be made downtown.

Although the Nugget has
been remodeled somewhat, it
still looks like a product of the
1970s, with more than a hint of
Graceland about its long, neat
rows of gold-painted lightbulbs,
little white leatherette stools
for slots players, and plump
white padded chairs
at the tables. About
the best thing you can
say about the casino
proper is that it's well
lit and high ceilinged.
Apart from the small
Buffet, the areas closest
to Fremont Street are
devoted to gambling.
Further back, the
Nugget built over an
entire block of Carson
Street, replacing it
with the disappointing
Carson Street Café
coffeeshop.

Genuine golden
nuggets displayed near
the lobby include the
Hand of Faith, the
largest in the world at
61lbs, 11oz. Found in

▲ THE GOLDEN NUGGET

▲ TYPICAL DECOR AT BINION'S HORSESHOE

Australia in 1980, it's now worth nearly half a million dollars.

Binion's Horseshoe

128 E Fremont St ☎ 800/622-6468, ⓦ www.binions.com. If the Golden Nugget represents downtown at its most pretentious, then Binion's Horseshoe goes to the other extreme, promoting itself as the definitive downtown gambling hall and nothing more. That hardnosed ethos dates back to its founder, Texas roughneck Benny Binion (see box below), who opened the Horseshoe as downtown's first "carpet joint" (as opposed to the rougher "sawdust joints" that had long characterized the area) in 1951. Although he turned the Horseshoe into the town's most profitable casino,

things went from bad to worse after his death in 1989. Binion's drug-addict son, Ted, was murdered in 1998 by his girlfriend and her new man, while his daughter Becky mismanaged the family finances so badly she first raided the casino's famous display case containing $1 million, and then in 2004 closed the place altogether. It reopened within months, and is currently being operated by Harrah's, widely believed to really be after the Horseshoe name and the World Series of Poker, established there in 1970. At the time of writing, the World Series was being held at the Rio, though it's expected that Harrah's will in due course build a new Horseshoe casino on the Strip, which would

The legend of Benny Binion

Benny Binion is affectionately remembered as one of the great Las Vegas characters, despite a record for violence that's exceptional even by local standards. An itinerant Texan horse-trader with at least two killings to his name, Benny ran the criminal underworld in Dallas during the 1940s, before a bloody gang feud persuaded him to relocate to Las Vegas. Acquiring two faltering Fremont Street casinos, he replaced them with the Horseshoe in 1951. Benny lost the casino when he was jailed for tax evasion in the 1950s – he finally learned to read and write while inside – and never regained his gaming license. However, his family bought the Horseshoe back in 1964, with Benny in charge behind the scenes. By the time he died, on Christmas Day 1989, the Horseshoe was the most profitable casino in Las Vegas.

▲ THE FOUR QUEENS

become a permanent home for the tournament.

What will become of the original Horseshoe remains to be seen. For the moment, it's in a somewhat sorry state, but the tables are still drawing in serious gamblers with some of the best odds and lowest minimums in town, and you can still get a great bargain meal downstairs at its atmospheric coffeeshop.

The Four Queens

202 E Fremont St ☎800/634-6045, ⓦwww.fourqueens.com. Named not for a poker hand but for the original owner's four daughters, the Four Queens has been a downtown fixture since 1966. In recent years it has spruced itself up, eschewing the old New Orleans theme in favor of matching the sparkling lights of the Golden Nugget. The one unusual feature of the otherwise staid Four Queens is that you're allowed to take photographs in the gaming area; just be sure to check with security personnel before you start.

The Fremont Hotel

200 E Fremont St ☎702/385-3232, ⓦwww.fremontcasino.com. When it was completed in 1956, the fifteen-story Fremont Hotel was the tallest building in Nevada. Its still-visible concrete facade was seen as shockingly modern, and marked a deliberate eschewal of downtown's previously universal Wild West architecture. Now owned by Sam Boyd of Sam's Town fame, the Fremont is these days just another downtown gambling palace, not quite as fashionable as the Golden Nugget but a little jazzier than the rest of the pack.

Fitzgeralds

301 E Fremont St ☎800/274-5825, ⓦwww.fitzgeraldslasvegas.com. Until recently, Fitzgeralds, which occupies an entire block of Fremont Street, was a tacky Irish-themed casino that sported every Celtic cliché imaginable, from leprechauns and shamrocks to a piece of the Blarney Stone. Owned since 2001 by Detroit businessman Don Barden – the first black person to own a casino in Nevada – it's been changing fast. The tired old Irish decor has almost entirely vanished, while new features include lots of free entertainment (including Elvis shows), a prominent *Krispy Kreme* outlet, and upgraded restaurants. The small balcony adjoining the second-floor lounge makes a good vantage point for watching the light show outside.

Neonopolis

450 E Fremont St ⓦwww.neonopolis .com. Sun–Thurs 11am–9pm, Fri & Sat 11am–10pm. What if they built a mall and nobody came? You might imagine the intersection of Fremont Street and Las Vegas Boulevard would be the perfect

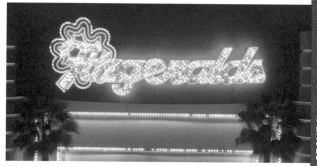

▲ FITZGERALDS

location to build a big new shopping mall and entertainment center. The city of Las Vegas certainly did. However, the block-long Neon-opolis mall has been a disaster since it opened in May 2002. Only a few tenants ever leased space, notably the fourteen-screen Crown movie theater (☎702/383-9600) and the *Jillian's* restaurant-cum-bowling alley (☎702/759-0450).

Half of a small ground-level souvenir store has been set aside as the disappointing **Las Vegas Gambling Museum** (Sun–Thurs 11am–9pm, Fri & Sat 11am–10pm; $2.50). The lackluster holdings include chips and matchbooks from scores of defunct casinos, display cases on Bugsy Siegel, Elvis Presley, and the Sands, and some truly dreadful waxworks of the Rat Pack. Most units in Neonopolis remain empty, however – there are only three outlets in the food court – and despite the location, just across the street from the Fremont Street Experience, the complex almost always seems to be empty.

El Cortez

600 E Fremont St ☎800/634-6703, ⓦwww.elcortez.net. Surrounded by pawn shops and T-shirt stores, a couple of rather uneasy blocks' walk east of the Fremont Street Experience, the shabby, quasi-Moorish El Cortez is downtown at its most downmarket. While the cut-rate rooms and suites make it a haunt of budget travelers, this casino stays in business due to its appeal to local low-rollers. As well as some of the lowest-stakes gambling in town, it also offers some of the lousiest, featuring regular drawings of Social Security numbers, with a $50,000 prize for matching all nine digits.

The Plaza

1 Main St ☎800/634-6575, ⓦwww.plazahotelcasino.com. The giant Plaza casino faces the west end of Fremont Street from the site of Las Vegas's now-defunct railroad station. After Amtrak abandoned rail service here in 1997, its facilities were absorbed into the Plaza's capacious bowels, but Greyhound buses continue to use the adjoining depot. Despite recent renovations, the Plaza is still aimed primarily at low-stakes gamblers, with its 2¢ slots, $1 blackjack tables, and a large Race and Sports Book that's forever busy with off-duty local employees and Greyhound passengers.

The Neon Museum

Las Vegas is seldom sentimental about erasing its past, but as casino after casino eschews "vulgar" neon in favor of "classy" gilt trimmings and LEDs, dewy-eyed preservationists have campaigned to save its abandoned neon glories. As a result, the block of Fremont Street alongside Neonopolis has been grandly designated as the **Neon Museum** (⊛ www.neonmuseum.org). Around a dozen restored neon signs are on show, including the Horse and Rider from the Hacienda, which was demolished to make way for Mandalay Bay, and the original magic lamp from the old Aladdin. The museum hopes in due course to open a two-acre outdoor "Neon Boneyard" of unrestored signs at 770 Las Vegas Blvd N.

Main Street Station

200 N Main St ☎ 800/851-1703, ⊛ www.mainstreetcasino.com. Despite unpromising beginnings – it went broke within a year of opening in 1991 – Main Street Station (not part of the Stations chain of casinos scattered around the city) has turned into a rare downtown success story. Standing two blocks off Fremont Street, and benefiting from a tasteful design intended to evoke New Orleans in the 1890s, it boasts a well-thought-out array of good-value, down-to-earth restaurants and other facilities. Although the theming is pleasant enough, however, with its polished wooden paneling and

▲ THE NEON MUSEUM

appealing *fin-de-siècle* railroad fittings, there simply isn't anything here to make it that exciting.

California Hotel

12 Ogden Ave ☎ 702/388-2665, ⊛ www.thecal.com. The California Hotel is a run-of-the-mill downtown casino notable solely for the fact that it's heavily dominated by Hawaiian customers. Sam Boyd (who also owns the neighboring Main Street Station) named it thus in 1975 in the understandable expectation that most of the clientele would be Californian. He soon turned his attention to Hawaii, however, where he had run bingo games in his youth, and that scheme proved very successful. It's a pleasant enough, if very low-profile place, with Hawaiian menu items prominent in the bars and restaurants, and where even the slot machines are labeled in Hawaiian.

Lied Discovery Children's Museum

833 Las Vegas Blvd N ☎ 702/384-3445, ⊛ www.ldcm.org. Daily 10am–5pm, closed Mon in winter. $7, under-18s $6. The Lied Discovery Children's Museum, housed in a library a mile north of downtown, is far less likely to stimulate childish imaginations than the wonders on the

Strip. Local school kids enjoy the chance to paint, draw, and sculpt, but even the youngest tourists may resent being dragged away from Luxor or Circus Circus. Many exhibits are sponsored by casinos, so visitors can hit white pipes like the Blue Men, or learn how neon signs work. However, the more sophisticated displays are often broken, so unless a good temporary exhibition is taking place there's not much point coming all the way up here.

Las Vegas Natural History Museum

900 Las Vegas Blvd N ☎ 702/384-3466, ⓦ www.lvnhm.org. Daily 9am–4pm. $6 adults, $5 ages 12–18, $3 ages 3–11. A block north of the children's museum, the Las Vegas Natural History Museum at least tries to move beyond the standard dioramas of stuffed animals. Thus the Marine Life Room features a smallish tank of live sharks alongside its mocked-up whales, while the Prehistoric Room offers five large animatronic monsters, including a roaring Tyrannosaurus Rex. Even the old-fashioned exhibits in the Africa section downstairs are less static than you might expect; note the zebra frantically trying to fend off two lions.

Restaurants

Andre's

401 S 6th St ☎ 702/385-5016, ⓦ www.andrelv.com. Dinner only, closed Sun. Of downtown's few gourmet restaurants, *Andre's* is the only one not in a casino. It's housed instead in a former private home, styled to resemble an antique-furnished French country inn. The ingredients

▲ ANDRE'S

are drawn from all over the world, from Australian lobsters to Maryland crabs, but the cuisine is classic French – and so are the prices, with the appetizers averaging around $15 and many entrees, like the broiled Berkshire pork chop, well over $30. Don't expect a low-cal experience, because whether you go for red meat in a thick fruity sauce, or fish swimming in butter, you've still got the impossibly rich desserts to contend with. *Andre's* has another branch in the Monte Carlo on the Strip.

The Coffee Shop

Binion's Horseshoe, 128 E Fremont St ☎ 702/382-1600. Daily 24hr. The round-the-clock Las Vegas coffeeshop of your dreams, located deep inside Binion's Horseshoe. The food is American-diner-heaven, with excellent prices for a changing timetable of specials. Best bargains are to be had in the dead of night (11pm–7am), when a steak dinner, with two eggs and magnificent home fries, costs just $6, and half that if you swap sausages for steak. Breakfast, which works out better value than most buffets, is served 24hr, while $7 Chinese specials are available for lunch and dinner.

Second Street Grill

The Fremont Hotel, 200 E Fremont St ☎702/385-3232. Dinner only, closed Tues & Wed. Downtown's most original fine-dining option, an up-to-the-minute "Pacific Rim" restaurant that occupies a disappointingly dull wood-paneled room near the Fremont's front door. The influence of consulting Hawaiian master chef Jean Marie Josselin (the culinary mind behind *8-0-8* in Caesars), is apparent throughout the pan-Asian menu, which draws heavily on Chinese, Thai, and Japanese traditions. Appetizers, costing $11–15, are largely seafood-oriented, including *ahi* sashimi and crab cakes; of the meat entrees, there are steaks for $22–25 or Chinese duck with blackberry glaze for $23, while a whole wok-fried catfish is $27.

ZAX

The Golden Nugget, 129 E Fremont St ☎702/385-7111. Dinner only.

Although the shortage of genuine fine dining downtown spurred the Golden Nugget to replace its *California Pizza Kitchen* with this contemporary American restaurant, the conversion seems strangely half-hearted, with its funky multicolored light fixtures and chrome columns rather spoiled by stale carpets and veneer paneling. The layout is similarly mixed-up: even though *ZAX* is part supper club, with a lounge singer crooning the likes of *Lady In Red*, you can't see the stage from many of the tables. The food itself is dependable but a little dull, with starters such as oysters gratin ($9) and tuna tartare with shiitake mushrooms ($13), followed by entrees ranging from roasted pork tenderloin ($23) up to steak ($38).

Buffets

Garden Court Buffet

Main Street Station, 200 N Main St ☎702/387-1896. Breakfast $6, lunch $8, dinner Mon, Wed, Sat & Sun $11,

▼ SECOND STREET GRILL

Tues & Thurs $13, Fri $16. This spacious dining room features attractive brickwork and cast iron, and plenty of natural light by day. Everything is clean and spruce, but not all that thrilling, with dishes ranging from fried chicken and corn in the "South by Southwest" section, to tortillas at "Olé," and pork chow mein and oyster tofu at "Pacific Rim." The salad selection is weak, and there's little fish overall except on specialty nights: Tuesday is T-Bone, Thursday is filet and scampi, and Friday is seafood.

Golden Nugget Buffet

The Golden Nugget, 129 E Fremont St ☎702/385-7111. Breakfast $7, lunch $8, dinner $13; Sun all-day champagne brunch $14. With its gold chandeliers and low mirrored ceiling, the Golden Nugget's buffet is presumably meant to look elegant; in fact it's small and claustrophobic. There's not much room for a kitchen, either, so while the salad bar is excellent, the choice of cooked food is limited. What there is, however – especially at the carving station – isn't bad, and the casino-front location is a definite advantage.

Buffet and Cafe

Fremont Hotel, 200 Fremont St ☎702/385-3232. Breakfast $6, lunch $6.50; dinner Mon & Thurs $10, Tues, Fri & Sun $15, Wed & Sat $12. This tropical-themed buffet is a classic slice of old-style downtown Vegas "glamour," all splashing water, glitter, and artificial plants. As a rule, the food is dependable, but much the best time to come is for the pricier "Seafood Fantasy" on Tuesday, Friday, and Sunday evenings, when the plates are piled high with crabs, lobsters, and raw oysters, plus scampi and steamed mussels. Wednesday and Saturday are steak nights. For those with smaller appetites, it's also possible to order à la carte, with soup such as the Hawaiian noodle *saimin* for $5, and sandwiches for $6.

Bars and lounges

Triple 7 Brewpub

Main Street Station, 200 N Main St ☎702/386-4442. Daily 11am–7am. The service at this roomy, high-ceilinged downtown brewpub can be slow, but the beers are great, the food tasty (as well as pizzas, burgers, and ribs, they sell shrimp in vast quantities), and there's often live entertainment as well.

Shows

Downtown Gordie Brown

The Golden Nugget, 129 E Fremont St ☎702/386-8100. Mon & Sun 7.30pm, Tues, Fri & Sat 7.30pm & 9.30pm. $55. From the moment the curtain rises in the unexciting showroom, revealing a funky seven-piece band ready to follow his every cue, this young, energetic impersonator has the audience roaring. Though some of his targets are a little tired – Forrest Gump, Jimmy Stewart, Neil Diamond – and his intricate mix of script and ad-libs is often lost in the general hullabaloo, Brown's enthusiasm is infectious. He specializes in quick-fire duos, like a fight between Ozzy Osbourne and Bob Dylan, or Elton John coping with a drunk Billy Joel. And it never hurts to use Elvis to bring things to a crescendo.

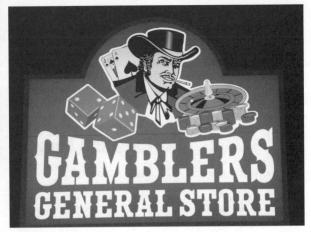

▲ GAMBLERS GENERAL STORE

Shops

The Attic
1018 S Main St ☎702/388-4088,
ⓦwww.theatticlasvegas.com. Mon–
Thurs 10am–5pm, Fri 10am–6pm,
Sat 11am–6pm. Located in an
insalubrious area about ten
blocks south of Fremont, this
shrine to vintage Americana
– both chic and kitsch – stocks
some amazing stuff, though it's
too cannily priced to allow you
to leave with your arms full.
Clothes and costumes range
from old Levi's and bell-bottoms
to flamboyant 1960s creations,
plus great shoes, hats, and accessories. The furniture is a delight
as well, including items like
turquoise vinyl armchairs, and
there's also a little coffee bar.

Gamblers General Store
800 S Main St ☎702/382-9903
or 800/322-2447, ⓦwww
.gamblersgeneralstore.com. Daily
9am–5pm. The perfect place

for a truly authentic Las Vegas
souvenir, a few blocks south
of downtown. As well as old
slot machines for $999 and a
full-sized craps table for $4000,
they sell felt mats with roulette,
blackjack, and craps layouts for
$40, and casino playing cards for
99¢. There's also a large library
of books on gambling, detailing
techniques for blackjack, craps,
horses, and even slots – if you
don't mind paying $20 for a
photocopied pamphlet explain-
ing why you'll never win.

Wedding chapels

Graceland Wedding Chapel
619 Las Vegas Blvd S ☎702/382-0091
or 800/824-5732, ⓦwww
.gracelandchapel.com. Although
this King-themed chapel will
provide you with an Elvis
impersonator to act as best man,
give the bride away, or even
serenade you, he unfortunately
can't perform the service itself.

West of the Strip

Las Vegas may look enormous on the map, but as far as visitors are concerned, the only significant neighborhoods are the Strip and downtown. No other area is likely to tempt you out of your car, let alone merit an excursion on public transport. With the exception of the Rio and Palms casinos, both half a mile off the Strip, your only conceivable ports of call in western Las Vegas are a low-key museum and the various scattered "locals casinos." Aimed primarily at local gamblers, the latter tend to hold bowling or skating facilities and movie theaters rather than white tigers and sphinxes, but with their good-value restaurants and low-stakes gambling they do at least have something to offer the out-of-state visitor.

The Rio

3700 W Flamingo Rd ☎800/752-9746, ⓦwww.playrio.com. Despite being stranded half a mile west of the Strip on the other side of I-15, the Rio established itself as a major Las Vegas player in the first few years after it opened in 1990. Although hailed at the time in magazine polls as the world's best-value hotel, a decade and a half on it has definitely sunk back into the pack. Now owned by Harrah's, the Rio still boasts a fine array of restaurants, plus big-name shows such as Penn and Teller, but it's lost much of the cachet that formerly lured visitors away from the Strip.

The Rio's most impressive feature remains its dramatic black-glass exterior and the stunning purple light show (visible from all over the city) that plays across both its original building and the newer hotel tower. In turn, the top of that tower, occupied by the *VooDoo*

Lounge, makes a great vantage point for viewing the Strip.

Inside, the "Rio" theme is tricky to pin down, having mutated from being specifically Brazilian to incorporating pretty much anything that's either tropical, carnival-related, or at the very least colorful. The **Masquerade Village** section stages its own twelve-minute "carnival" every two hours between 4pm and 10pm, in which parade "floats" suspended from overhead rails pass above the casino floor while costumed loons cavort on the central stage – occasionally, those few people not gambling will actually watch. In addition, the unfortunate

▼ THE RIO

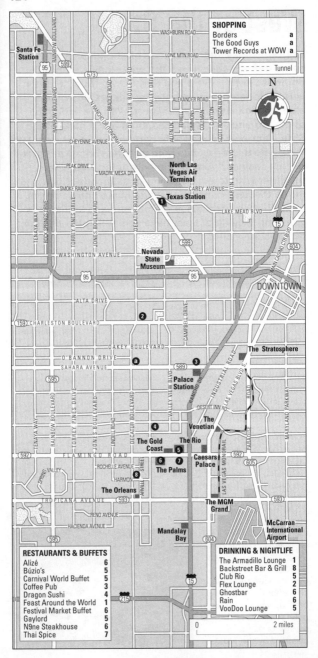

SHOPPING

Borders	a
The Good Guys	a
Tower Records at WOW	a

- - - - - Tunnel

North Las Vegas Air Terminal

Texas Station **1**

Nevada State Museum

DOWNTOWN

The Stratosphere

a

Palace Station **3**

The Venetian

Dragon Sushi **4**

The Gold Coast

The Rio

Caesars Palace

5

6 **7** The Palms

8

The Orleans

The MGM Grand

McCarran International Airport

Mandalay Bay

RESTAURANTS & BUFFETS

Alizé	6
Búzio's	5
Carnival World Buffet	5
Coffee Pub	3
Dragon Sushi	4
Feast Around the World	1
Festival Market Buffet	5
Gaylord	5
N9ne Steakhouse	6
Thai Spice	7

DRINKING & NIGHTLIFE

The Armadillo Lounge	1
Backstreet Bar & Grill	8
Club Rio	5
Flex Lounge	2
Ghostbar	6
Rain	5
VooDoo Lounge	5

0   2 miles

cocktail waitresses have been restyled as "bevertainers," and now sing as they deliver drinks to gamblers. In 2005, Harrah's made a move towards attracting the crowds back from the Strip by making the Rio a temporary home for the **World Series of Poker** (see p.173), but it's expected that the tournament will eventually move to a permanent home on the Strip.

The Palms

4321 W Flamingo Rd ☎866/942-7777, ⓦwww.palms.com. The Palms casino, which opened in 2001, has been a wildly successful experiment in appealing to both hip, high-rolling tourists and canny, cost-conscious locals. Thanks to the aggressive marketing campaign of owner George Maloof (whose family also owns the Sacramento Kings pro basketball team), it also ranks among Las Vegas's top celebrity hangouts.

While the Palms' closest equivalents are probably Mandalay Bay and the Hard Rock, both of which attract a similarly cool, young crowd, its most obvious rival – the Rio – stands just a few yards away, across Flamingo Road. It outdoes its neighbor by being just one story taller – though it should be noted that the Palms calls its

topmost 42nd floor its "55th," on the basis that for "good luck" it doesn't have a fourth, a thirteenth, or indeed anything from forty to forty-nine (the last being for the benefit of its Chinese guests). Other weapons in the Palms' arsenal include two nightclubs – the water-themed *Rain* and the penthouse ultra-lounge *Ghostbar* – a batch of very classy restaurants, and a deluxe spa.

Elements designed to please the locals market, on the other hand, include ample parking space, a fourteen-screen movie theater, and an abundance of (allegedly "loose") video poker machines. Indeed, the Palms is almost two distinct buildings, with the modern, trendier areas all congregated to the east side, and the less showy parts to the west.

The Gold Coast

4000 W Flamingo Rd ☎888/402-6278, ⓦwww.goldcoastcasino.com. The Gold Coast is much more of a locals casino than its two higher-profile neighbors, the Rio and the Palms. Though built only four years before the Rio, in 1986, with its old-style Western decor it has always had the feel of a much earlier era. In truth, it's not a bad little place, offering some cheap restaurants

PLACES West of the Strip

▼ THE PALMS

and a smoke-free section in the casino, plus the 70-lane Brunswick bowling alley upstairs and the two-screen movie theater downstairs. Free shuttle buses connect the Gold Coast to its owner's other two properties, the Orleans, not far to the southwest, and Barbary Coast on the Strip.

▲ TEXAS STATION

Nevada State Museum

700 Twin Lakes Drive ☎702/486-5205. Daily 9am–5pm. $2, under-18s free. The Nevada State Museum is both hard to find – follow Washington Avenue three miles west of downtown to Valley View Boulevard, then look for signs to Lorenzi Park – and hardly worth finding. Despite ample floor space, and a potentially fascinating subject in the history of the Las Vegas valley ever since it was roamed by mammoths, its displays are perfunctory and lifeless, aimed at school parties with short attention spans. What's more, the chronology peters out altogether in the 1950s, right when things start to get really interesting; the only glimpse you get of contemporary Las Vegas is a door once used by Bugsy Siegel – quite the dullest door you ever saw.

The Orleans

4500 W Tropicana Ave ☎800/675-3267, ⓦwww.orleanscasino.com. Two miles west of the Strip, a stylish facade of pastel-painted townhouses and balconies conceals the warehouse-like Orleans casino. For some gamblers, it's quite an exciting place, with low stakes on all table games, and video poker galore. Just don't expect too much from its New Orleans theme. The three jazz-playing alligators by the main doors typify the Orleans' half-hearted nods to Crescent City ambience,

with standard, middle-of-the-road stars rather than New Orleans musicians dominating its lounges and showrooms. It also holds a 70-lane, 24-hour bowling alley, and an eighteen-screen movie theater.

Palace Station

2411 W Sahara Ave ☎800/634-3101, ⓦwww.palacestation.com. The oldest of the Stations chain of local casinos, Palace Station (dating from 1976) is also the closest to the Strip, less than a mile west along Sahara Avenue. Although now feeling more claustrophobic and less appealing than its younger siblings, Palace still features the winning combination of inexpensive restaurants and emphasis on slots that established the chain's formula for success.

Santa Fe Station

4949 N Rancho Drive ☎866/767-7771, ⓦwww.stationcasinos.com. Santa Fe Station is a small locals casino in the far northwestern corner of town. Its Southwestern theming is minimal, though the dealers do at least wear bolo ties. The only reason that you might call in here – other than to make a pit stop en route to Mount Charleston – is to use its ice rink or 24-hour bowling alley.

Texas Station

2101 Texas Star Lane ☎800/654-8888, ⓦwww.texasstation.com.

The third in the Stations chain, built two miles northwest of downtown in 1995, Texas Station offers no outstanding novelties or gimmicks, but as locals casinos go it's definitely one of the best. "Texas" might not sound like a wildly exciting concept, and in truth the theming doesn't extend beyond enabling its guests to eat well, drink a lot, and gamble themselves into penury in cheerful surroundings. Besides an eighteen-screen movie theater, Texas Station has an enormous play area for kids (prices from $6/hr), as well as a separate, and very serious, Bingo Hall.

Restaurants

Alizé

The Palms, 4321 W Flamingo Rd ☏702/951-7000, ⓦwww.alizelv .com. Dinner only. *Alizé's* absolutely stunning, sky-high setting in the Palms, with glass walls to provide unobstructed Strip views, is easily matched by the exquisite (and correspondingly expensive) French-influenced cuisine, courtesy of André Rochat (of *André's* fame). Appetizers, soups, and salads start at $10, while the elaborate entrees, festooned with fascinating sides, can easily top $40. Specialties include the "four ways" rabbit for $35, and a hazelnut-crusted lamb chop with a green-pea crêpe for $42.

The Búzio's

Rio, 3700 W Flamingo Rd ☏702/252-7697. This smart, deli-like European seafood restaurant is separated by a long stretch of plate-glass window from the Rio's beach-like kids' swimming pool and waterfall, while its other flank is occupied by an open kitchen with counter seating. There's nothing very fancy about the cooking, but it is consistently good, with typical fish entrees for $16–20 at lunch, and a bit more at dinner, when you can also get substantial stews such as a $24 *cioppino* or a $27 *bouillabaisse* with lobster. The raw bar is half price at lunchtime, meaning a dozen oysters or clams costs $10.

Coffee Pub

2800 W Sahara Ave ☏702/367-1913. Daily breakfast and lunch. Large, bright, and rather upmarket coffeehouse, tucked into a small modern mall. Few of its clientele, drawn from the surrounding banks and offices, have the time to linger, but it's a nice enough place to sit, and has some outdoor seating. As well as specialty coffees and baked goods, the breakfast menu includes *huevos rancheros* or eggs Benedict for around $8; lunchtime salads, deli sandwiches, burgers, and pizzas cost slightly more.

▼ ALIZÉ

▲ DRAGON SUSHI, AT CHINA TOWN PLAZA

Dragon Sushi

China Town Plaza, 4115 W Spring Mountain Rd ☎702/368-4336. Good if not exceptional sushi at $5–8 per piece, plus noodle entrees at around $10, served in an intimate, friendly mall restaurant where individual, private Japanese-style dining rooms are also available.

Gaylord

Rio, 3700 W Flamingo Rd ☎702/777-2277, ⓦwww.gaylords.com. Dinner nightly, plus brunch Fri–Sun. With its smart setting, fine silverware, and formal service, *Gaylord* is much the classiest Indian restaurant in Las Vegas. That's reflected by the set menu prices, which start at $40 for the vegetarian option and range up to $50. Chicken dishes like *tikka masala* cost around $20, lamb more like $25, and vegetarian sides such as the

deliciously cheesy *mattar paneer* around $15. Weekend lunch-times there's an all-you-can-eat champagne brunch.

N9ne Steakhouse

The Palms, 4321 W Flamingo Rd ☎702/993-9900, ⓦwww.n9negroup .com. Dinner only. Assuming money's no object, Las Vegas's first outpost of the Chicago steak specialists is just the place to make you feel pampered and special. Its opulent features include a central champagne and caviar bar, a double-sided water wall, a ceiling that changes color, and a private celebrity dining area with glass walls so the rest of us can peer in. The menu, naturally, centers on steaks – all, from the 12oz filet mignon to the 24oz bone-in rib eye, cost around $40 – but you can also get a Kobe beef burger with fries for $25, plus assorted seafood appetizers and entrees. Expect a hefty check; even the vegetable sides cost $9 a throw.

Thai Spice

4433 W Flamingo Rd at I-15 ☎702/362-5308. Closed Sun. Some of Las Vegas's finest Thai food, served in a setting that's clean,

▼ GAYLORD

cheerful, and modern (though anonymous) opposite the Rio. Noodle dishes such as pad thai are reasonably priced and very tasty, and the soups are also pretty good. Lunchtime specials are excellent value at $6 or so, while even a full dinner works out under $20.

Buffets

Carnival World Buffet

Rio, 3700 W Flamingo Rd ☎702/252-7777. Breakfast $13, lunch $15, dinner $23. Even if the prices are not what they were, the Rio's revamped buffet remains just about the best value in any major casino, and is still able to lure bargain-hunting tourists away from the Strip. The variety is immense, including Thai, Chinese, Mexican, and Japanese stations – the latter does good sushi – as well as the usual pasta and barbecue options, and even a fish'n'chips stand. Desserts are also great, with plenty of sugar-free ones for all the good they'll do you. The only real drawback is that the lines are invariably long. Note that the Rio also has the separate and more expensive *Village Seafood Buffet*, offering highly recommended dinners for $35.

Feast Around The World

Texas Station, 2101 Texas Star Lane ☎702/631-1000. Breakfast $6, lunch $7, dinner Sun–Thurs $9, Fri & Sat $13. Texas Station lures in locals with the same attractive and very competitively priced buffet as its stablemate Sunset Station, as reviewed in full on p.140.

Festival Market Buffet

The Palms, 4321 W Flamingo Rd ☎702/942-7777. Breakfast $6, lunch $7, dinner Sat–Thurs $12, Fri $16. Easy to find – right in the middle of the casino, in full view of the gambling action – and easy to afford, the Palms' buffet has rapidly established itself as a local favorite. Food and decor alike are bright and appealing without being fancy, with a broad spectrum that takes in salads, a little sushi, Mexican and Italian specialties, teriyaki chicken, barbecue beef, and a lot of lovely cakes and pies. Prices rise on Friday night for the crab legs and prime rib special.

Bars and lounges

Backstreet Bar & Grill

5012 S Arville St ☎702/876-1844. Daily 24hr. This very friendly, gay-oriented country bar caters to both men and women and is home to Nevada's Gay Rodeo Association (see p.179). Square dancing on Tuesday evenings, line dancing on Thursdays (beginners welcome), country dancing on Fridays and Saturdays, and an almighty beer bust on Sunday afternoons.

Ghostbar

The Palms, 4321 W Flamingo Rd ☎702/940-7777, ⓦwww .ghostbar.com. Daily 8pm–dawn.

▼ FESTIVAL MARKET BUFFET

▲ RAIN

Cover Sun–Thurs $10, Fri & Sat $20. Self-proclaimed "ultra-lounge" on what the Palms calls its 55th story; the lack of a dance floor and the low volume of the music means that it can't quite be categorized as a nightclub, but it's a major celeb hangout. Thirty-something hipsters wait in line to pay the cover charge, then venture out to enjoy the views from its cantilevered open-air deck, which has a terrifying, vertigo-inducing plexiglass floor.

VooDoo Lounge

The Rio, 3700 W Flamingo Rd ☎702/252-7777. Daily 11am–3am. Cover $10 and up. A few years have passed since the 51st-floor *VooDoo Lounge* was Las Vegas's hottest bar, but tourists and locals alike still happily wait in line to experience its super-cool atmosphere and the amazing Strip views from its outdoor terrace. Inside, the purple-tinted windows make it hard to see out, but most of the self-consciously beautiful crowd prefer to admire their own reflections anyway. The ersatz New Orleans voodoo-themed decor, and the "mixologists" diligently setting cocktails aflame, add to the ambience, there's live music nightly except Mondays, and the food is pretty good, too. No T-shirts or sneakers.

Clubs and music venues

The Armadillo Lounge

Texas Station, 2101 Texas Star Lane ☎702/631-8275, ⓦ www.texasstation .com. Every Friday and Saturday night, this atmospheric lounge fills with dressed-up locals for a wild Eighties party, featuring the cover band Love Shack and watched over by a 200-pound mirrored disco armadillo.

Club Rio

The Rio, 3700 W Flamingo Rd ☎702/252-7777. Wed–Sat 10.30pm–4am. Men $10, women $5. Upmarket, relatively staid dance club that takes over the Rio's large circular showroom after hours to play mainly Eighties music – though it's Latin-influenced house on Wednesdays, and wider-ranging dance tunes on Thursdays – to a predominantly thirty-plus throng.

Flex Lounge

4371 W Charleston Blvd ☎702/385-3539. Daily 24hr. Cover up to $5. Flamboyant gay club with an emphasis on music and dancing as opposed to drinking, and occasional strip shows. Beer flows freely all week, with DJs Wed–Sat, and Mon set aside for karaoke.

Rain

The Palms, 4321 W Flamingo Rd ☎702/940-7246, ⓦ www .rainatthepalms.com. Thurs 11pm–5am

$10, Fri & Sat 10pm–5am $20. This glitzy, water-themed dance club is currently the hottest celebrity hangout in town, thanks to its fabulous decor – fountains of water and fire – huge dance floor, and plush, private VIP areas. When it's warm enough, the action spreads into the outdoors area around the pool. Expect to wait an hour or more to be allowed in. No shorts or sneakers.

Shows

Penn & Teller

Samba Theatre, The Rio, 3700 W Flamingo Rd ☎ 702/777-7776, ⓦ www .pennandteller.com. Nightly except Tues 9pm. $77. Having long since established themselves as alternative, even iconoclastic magicians, Penn & Teller are now several years into a Rio residency that they "don't like to think of as a typical Las Vegas show." Which begs the question, given that they're charging Las Vegas prices, what is it then? While their schtick of deconstructing classic magic tricks to show how they're done is interesting, it's hardly electrifying. They do perform a number of set-piece stunts undeniably well, but the pacing of the show is frankly rather flat, and Penn Jillette's endless patter, when not truculent, seems merely complacent. If you're a fan already, you'll probably love them; if not, don't bother.

Shops

Borders

2323 S Decatur Blvd ☎ 258-0999. Mon–Sat 9am–11pm, Sun 9am–9pm. An excellent range of new books and magazines at this sizable, better-than-average chain store along Sahara Avenue. Other branches at 2190 N Rainbow Blvd (across from Barnes & Noble) and 1445 W Sunset Rd in Henderson (near Sunset Station).

The Good Guys

4580 W Sahara Ave ☎ 364-2500, ⓦ www.thegoodguys.com. Daily 9am–midnight. The best source in Las Vegas for well-priced electronic goods of all kinds, from computers and cameras to TVs and audio equipment. Also at Boulevard Mall (see p.143).

Tower Records at WOW

4580 W Sahara Ave ☎ 364-2500. Daily 10am–midnight. A couple of blocks east of Borders, Tower boasts a good collection of new CDs – with a better chance of finding a bargain than at Virgin – and forms part of a larger complex that also sells videos and musical equipment.

PLACES West of the Strip

▼ BORDERS

East of the Strip

Las Vegas is somewhat less amorphous east of the Strip than it is to the west, with certain clusters at least sporting distinct characteristics. Thus Paradise Road, parallel to the Strip, holds several good restaurants and bars (mainly around Twain Avenue), and also provides a focus for the city's gay scene in the bars and clubs in the so-called "Fruit Loop," south of the Hard Rock. Thanks to the proximity of the University of Nevada, Las Vegas (UNLV), Maryland Parkway east of Paradise is the epicenter of the "University District," lined with cafes, budget restaurants, and cheap book and music stores. Slightly further north you'll find the sprawling Boulevard shopping mall. The wealthy, mushrooming suburb of Henderson is another half-dozen miles southwest.

Las Vegas Hilton

3000 Paradise Rd ☎888/732-7117, ⓦwww.lvhilton.com. Half a mile east of the Strip, alongside the Convention Center, the Las Vegas Hilton was for its first eight years the city's most prestigious resort. A month after opening as the International in 1969, it hosted Elvis Presley's triumphant return to live performance – the King went on to sell out 837 consecutive shows, ultimately appearing in front of 2.5 million people (the hotel's Elvis connection is commemorated by a gilt statue in the main lobby). Given such a successful beginning, it seemed possible for a time that the Hilton might spearhead the development of Paradise Road as a second, parallel, Strip. This never really happened, and it took 25 years for Paradise Road to acquire its second casino, the Hard Rock. While the Strip boomed, the Hilton became the

▲ LAS VEGAS HILTON

casino that Las Vegas forgot, depending for its survival on business travelers attracted by its proximity to the Convention Center next door. It was ultimately absorbed into the Caesars empire, who shunted its former high-rolling regulars to their other proper-

▲ HARD ROCK HOTEL

ties. The Hilton's prospects may be on the upswing, though, now that it has its own Monorail station to bring in customers from the Strip. The gamblers who come out this way appreciate the glitzy gaming area, not to mention the world's largest, and probably most elaborate, Race and Sports Book.

Gambling aside, the most obvious attraction for casual visitors is the **Star Trek Experience** (Sun–Thurs 11am–10pm, Fri & Sat 11am–11pm, rides slightly shorter hours; ⓦwww.startrekexp.com; $35, under-13s $32), housed in the Hilton's North Tower and roughly equivalent to a top-echelon ride in an LA or Orlando theme park; it's pretty good, but absurdly expensive. Visits start from the Space Quest Casino, a sort of *Enterprise* with slots. The ramp beyond the ticket booths doubles as a queuing area – you can wait as long as two hours on summer weekends – and a "museum," where glossy display panels recount a wordy episode-by-episode chronology of every *Star Trek* series. Artifacts and costumes abound, with diminutive Ferengi strolling among you. The whole thing culminates in two separate twenty-minute shows: *Klingon Encounter* and *Borg Invasion 4-D*, both of which

involve being caught up in alien plots and sent on vomit-inducing motion-simulator rides through deep space. You eventually emerge in a shopping area (which you actually could have reached without paying) where memorabilia prices boldly go to well over $2000 for a customized leather jacket. The adjoining *Quark Bar*, with its deep-space decor and inter-galactic cocktails, makes a fun place to recuperate.

Hard Rock Hotel

4455 Paradise Rd ☎800/473-7625, ⓦwww.hardrockhotel.com. If you don't already share the delusion that the *Hard Rock Cafe* is by definition the coolest place in any city worldwide, little about the Hard Rock Hotel, a mile east of the Strip, is likely to convince you. Its brochures drone on about how "hip" the place is, and how it's "the first ever rock'n'roll resort," but ultimately the place is not a patch on the Strip giants. Yes, guitars signed by the likes of Bob Dylan and George Michael hang above the check-in desk, and the cashier's cage bears the slogan "In Rock We Trust." Elsewhere, mannequins sport Prince's spangly jumpsuit and Madonna's pointy corset, while motorcycles and drum kits stand atop slot machines. Killing the whole

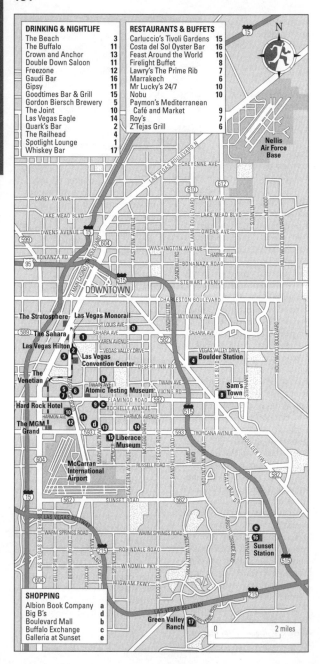

DRINKING & NIGHTLIFE

The Beach	3
The Buffalo	11
Crown and Anchor	13
Double Down Saloon	11
Freezone	12
Gaudí Bar	16
Gipsy	11
Goodtimes Bar & Grill	15
Gordon Biersch Brewery	5
The Joint	10
Las Vegas Eagle	14
Quark's Bar	2
The Railhead	4
Spotlight Lounge	1
Whiskey Bar	17

RESTAURANTS & BUFFETS

Carluccio's Tivoli Gardens	15
Costa del Sol Oyster Bar	16
Feast Around the World	16
Firelight Buffet	8
Lawry's The Prime Rib	7
Marrakech	6
Mr Lucky's 24/7	10
Nobu	10
Paymon's Mediterranean Café and Market	9
Roy's	7
Z'Tejas Grill	6

SHOPPING

Albion Book Company	a
Big B's	b
Boulevard Mall	c
Buffalo Exchange	d
Galleria at Sunset	e

rockin' fantasy, though, is the hard fact that the Hard Rock is just another hotel/casino, and rather a lame one at that, populated by pony-tailed men and designer-label women trying to look twenty years younger. Nothing about the place suggests "hard rock," not even the background music, which remains consistently soft and soothing.

▲ LIBERACE MUSEUM

Much smaller and easier to negotiate than its Strip counterparts – the casino takes up the sunken central floor of the circular building, so it can be neatly avoided if you wish – the Hard Rock is also as a rule much less busy. The guest rooms are so high-priced and few in number (relatively speaking), that the only time things really come alive here is when there's a big-name gig in *The Joint*. In fairness, the Hard Rock does boast a better-than-average line-up of musical acts, some great restaurants, and a showpiece pool, but it's not really worth going out of your way to see it.

The Atomic Testing Museum

755 E Flamingo Rd ☎702/794-5151, ⓦwww.ntshf.org. Mon–Sat 9am–5pm, Sun 11am–5pm. $10, seniors and students $7, under-6s free. This new offshoot of the Nevada Test Site Historical Foundation – which preserves history of the nearby desert location where nuclear weapons were tested from 1951 to 1992 – exhibits a mix of kitschy and serious artifacts, including nuclear-tinged pop-culture items, film clips, and a re-creation of a bomb shelter. There's also a library with hundreds of thousands of declassified documents. The

main attraction, however, is a full-sensory simulation of an above-ground nuclear explosion in the so-called "Ground Zero Theater."

Liberace Museum

1775 E Tropicana Ave ☎702/798-5595, ⓦwww.liberace.org. Mon–Sat 10am–5pm, Sun noon–4pm. Adults $12, students 6 and older $8. Las Vegas's finest museum is, not surprisingly, the one most in keeping with the city's sheer exhibitionism. The Liberace Museum, two miles east of the Strip, is a fabulous (if po-faced) romp through the life of Walter Liberace (1919–87), who was advised by fellow Polish musical maestro Paderewski to change his name to a single word.

Born in Wauwatosa, Wisconsin, Liberace started out playing five hours a night, six nights a week in Milwaukee in 1940 for $45. Within four years he was appearing in Las Vegas, and by 1954 he was earning $2 million for a 26-week season in New York.

With success came scandal – Liberace was ruthlessly hounded by the press – but also phenomenal wealth. His collection of pianos ranges from one played by Chopin for Liszt, to another shaped like a giraffe, while his displayed furnishings include a horrendous desk that belonged to the last czar of Russia, and his bedroom suite, equipped with two single beds.

Liberace is now remembered less for his music – which has not improved with age – than his costumes. He called them "a very expensive joke"; confronted by rhinestone-studded furs valued at $750,000, it's hard to disagree. The *pièce de résistance* is the red, white, and blue hot-pants set he wore for the Bicentennial in 1976. Said to have cost a million dollars, it looks worth ten bucks at the most.

Boulder Station

4111 Boulder Hwy ☎800/683-7777, ⓦwww.boulderstation.com. Boulder Station was the second in the Stations chain of locals casinos. While it lures in customers with the usual combination of cheap, cheerful restaurants, an eleven-screen movie theater, and childcare facilities ($6–7/hr), what sets this casino apart from its brethren is how seriously betting is taken here. The huge Race and Sports Book has a positively Dickensian atmosphere, with rows of pencil-chewing gamblers overlooked by

dark Victorian "stained glass" as they scan the news from far-off racetracks. Railroad motifs permeate the whole place, especially in the *Railhead* lounge.

Sam's Town

5111 Boulder Hwy ☎800/897-8696, ⓦwww.samstownlv.com. A last hold-out of Las Vegas's once-ubiquitous Wild West theme, Sam's Town, six miles east of the Strip, is the quintessential locals casino. After years of low-profile prosperity from providing bargain-basement grub-and-gambling, it has blossomed into a genuinely appealing place whose biggest downside is being so out of the way; see it while en route to or from the Hoover Dam.

While its general decor is still bursting with boots'n'spurs'n'cactuses, Sam's Town now centers on a bright, spacious glass-roofed atrium, officially known as Mystic Falls Park. Kitted out with fiberglass mountains, waterfalls, real trees, recorded birdsong, and even animatronic beavers, it's reminiscent – if you're in the right mood – of New York's Central Park. A free "Sunset Stampede" laser and light show

▲ BOULDER STATION

▲ SAM'S TOWN

takes place four times daily (2pm, 6pm, 8pm & 10pm). On the south side of the casino, the vast **Sam's Town Live** complex is an 1100-seat performance and dining space, most commonly hosting country entertainers. There's also an 18-screen movie theater and a 56-lane, 24-hour bowling center.

Sunset Station

1301 W Sunset Rd, Henderson ⓣ888/786-7389, ⓦwww.sunsetstation.com. Located opposite the Galleria Mall in suburban Henderson, Sunset Station is a long drive from central Las Vegas. Being located on the way to Hoover Dam, however, means it's not exactly off the beaten path, and it's a worthy destination in its own right. Completed in 1997, Sunset Station was designed to look something like an old Spanish mission. The attempt is enjoyable enough, even if it's not all that coherent, and some of the interior trimmings are truly spectacular. An extraordinary adobe-styled and mushroom-shaped canopy of stained and colored glass undulates above the gaming area, reaching a climax in the fantastic mosaic-enhanced *Gaudí Bar*. Sunset Station also features a thirteen-screen movie theater, some good restaurants and an excellent buffet, childcare facilities, and a games arcade, plus free shuttle buses to the Strip.

Green Valley Ranch

2300 Paseo Verde Parkway, Henderson ⓣ888/782-9487, ⓦwww.greenvalleyranchresort.com. Perched on rising ground eight miles southeast of the Strip in suburban Henderson, Green Valley Ranch opened in 2001 as the tenth, and by far most high-end, outpost in the ever-expanding Stations chain. Owner Frank Fertitta III said he was attempting to "create the perfect mouse trap," but it's not mice he wants to catch so much as big cheeses – high-spending, luxury-loving gamblers who don't want to stay on the Strip. Whether many such creatures actually exist is debatable, but with its extensive pools, spa, and panoramic gardens, Green Valley Ranch is certainly a well-laid trap. Local residents come for this chain's usual good-value buffet and the movie theater, as well as the restaurants, which are of a higher grade than in most Stations properties, with outlets such as *Il Fornaio* and *Border Grill*. The big-name attraction here for tourists, however, is definitely the no-expense-spared *Whiskey Bar* nightclub.

Restaurants

Carluccio's Tivoli Gardens

1775 E Tropicana Ave ⓣ702/795-3236. Dinner only, closed Mon. Conventional upscale Italian restaurant with an irresistible angle – it was designed by

▲ COSTA DEL SOL OYSTER BAR

Liberace himself, whose museum now stands next door. Hence the mirrored lounge and piano-shaped bar, not to mention the incongruity of the entire English pub he shipped over. The menu is wide ranging and consistently rich, with pizzas and chicken dishes at $10–12, and linguini with mussels for $14, but it's hard to resist Liberace's own personal favorite, the $8.50 baked lasagna.

Costa del Sol Oyster Bar

Sunset Station, 1301 W Sunset Rd ☎702/547-7777. Pleasant, spacious casino restaurant, sadly a long way off the Strip, that's encased in an undulating "grotto" complete with cascading waterfalls. Dishing out consistently good seafood, they serve up raw oysters or clams at $8 per half-dozen; steamed, with clams or New Zealand mussels at $13; in stews, like a French *bouillabaisse* or an Italian *cioppino*, for $17; or in a gumbo or roast, with crab, lobster, or shrimp, at around $16. For $13 you can also get six oyster shooters, each with a different liquor. The adjoining *Costa del Sol* restaurant serves an even longer menu for dinner, Wed–Sun only.

Lawry's The Prime Rib

4043 E Howard Hughes Parkway at Flamingo ☎702/893-2223, ✆www .lawrysonline.com. Dinner only. *Lawry's* has been a Beverly Hills tradition since 1938, but the Las Vegas branch only opened in 1997. Even so, it's a lovely, stylishly designed tribute to the Art Deco era, enhanced by flamboyant service. Prime rib is no longer (quite) the only thing on the menu ($25–40 per entree), but it's the only reason you'd bother to come here, and *Lawry's* juicy, generously-sized cuts may well be the best you've ever tasted.

Marrakech

Citibank Park, 3900 Paradise Rd ☎702/737-5611. Dinner only. All-you-can-eat banquets of rich Moroccan food, costing $30 per person and eaten with your fingers from low-lying tables around which you sit on scattered cushions. The tasty but very meaty couscous and pastry dishes are complemented by some unexpected seafood alternatives, and followed by heavy desserts. The main reason to come is to enjoy the faux-romantic Middle Eastern atmosphere, belly dancers and all, definitely not a place for a quick meal on your own.

Mr Lucky's 24/7

Hard Rock Hotel, 4455 Paradise Rd ☎702/693-5000. Daily 24hr. Oddly enough, the *Hard Rock Cafe* itself is not in the casino proper but out in the parking lot, so wannabes who want to soak up the atmosphere inside but can't afford the room rates have to hang out instead in *Mr Lucky's*, its 24-hour coffeeshop. With its open kitchen, faux-fur booths, and subdued tan-and-cream paint-job, this is actually a fairly classy place, and the food is well above average, too. As well as all the usual breakfast items, they serve burgers, sandwiches, pizzas, and pasta dishes for $7–12, a 12-oz steak for $18, and milkshakes or microbrews for $5.

Nobu

Hard Rock Hotel, 4455 Paradise Rd ☎702/693-5090, ⓦwww .nobumatsuhisa.com. Dinner only.
The Hard Rock, with its target audience of affluent Southern Californian would-be hipsters, makes an appropriate setting for one of Las Vegas's chic-est celebrity-thronged restaurants, run by Japanese-Peruvian chef Nobu Matsuhisa (as seen in New York, LA, and London). The decor is supremely tasteful, with individual walls of rounded river rocks and seaweed paper; the crowd is very upmarket; and with the temptation to keep ordering yet another morsel the prices tend to rocket before your eyes. The food, though, is exquisite, whether you simply go for the sushi bar, or select from the "special cold dishes" (three tiny oysters for $12, or salmon tartare with caviar at $25). Sushi or sashimi set dinners start at $30, with a "chef's choice" option for $65, or you can leave the whole thing up to the chef for $80 and up.

Paymon's Mediterranean Café and Market

Tiffany Square, 4147 S Maryland Parkway at Flamingo ☎702/731-6030, ⓦwww.paymons.com. Mon–Thurs 11am–1am, Fri & Sat 11am–3am, Sun 11am–3pm. This simple but highly recommended Middle Eastern restaurant – much easier to reach if you're heading south rather than north on Maryland – is Las Vegas's best vegetarian option. In most US cities that might make it an "alternative" hangout; here, despite

having the university nearby, *Paymon's* is just a popular and extremely affordable (but not very atmospheric) lunchtime rendezvous. The Cretan murals are attractive, though, the food is tasty and substantial, the service very friendly, and there's even a "hookah lounge" next door. Salads and pita sandwiches cost $7–9, and spinach pie $10, while dips such as *hummus* or the eggplant-based *baba ganoush* are $5. If you can't make up your mind, a mountainous best-of-everything combination plate is just $11. *Paymon's* has another branch in Summerlin at 8380 W Sahara Ave.

Roy's

620 E Flamingo Rd ☎702/691-2053, ⓦwww.roysrestaurant.com. Dinner only.
Thanks to its off-Strip location – rare indeed in Las Vegas for a big national name – *Roy's* sees far fewer tourists than locals, but for both food and ambience it's every bit the match of the top casino restaurants, with significantly lower prices to boot. Part of a gourmet chain that originated in Hawaii, it serves Asian-inspired fusion cuisine, specializing in fish. A melt-in-your-mouth miso butterfish appetizer costs $10, while entrees featuring Hawaiian species ($20–28) include lemongrass *opah*, macadamia-nut-crusted *ono*, and the irresistible whole *moi* or threadfish. Meat-eaters can get steak, veal, or lamb

▲ LAWRY'S THE PRIME RIB

▲ FIRELIGHT BUFFET

for similar prices, while a set meal with a mixed sampler appetizer, meat or fish entree, and dessert, goes for $30. There's another *Roy's* eight miles west of the Strip in residential Summerlin, at 8701 W Charleston Blvd (☎702/838-3620).

Z'Tejas Grill

3824 Paradise Rd at Twain ☎702/732-1660, ✆www.ztejas.com. Despite its tiresome name – taken, apparently, from a former chef's mispronunciation of "The Texas Grill" – and its overblown repu-tation for "daring," the food at *Z'Tejas Grill* is good and afford-able enough to merit venturing a mile off the Strip. The vaguely Southwestern cuisine takes in everything from New Orleans to the Pacific, and down to Mexico, too. The appetizers are the most interesting part; in fact, you could easily skip the main plates of chicken burritos, catfish tacos and the like, for a meal of start-ers like the seared and peppered sesame tuna, or the sushi-esque grilled and chilled seafood roll. At around $10, each costs roughly the same as the entrees, anyway, and is just as substantial; what's more, starters are half price during the weekday happy hour, 4–7pm. There's an outdoor patio, which is a little close to the road but at least offers a bit of fresh air after being cooped up in all those casinos.

Buffets

Feast Around The World

Sunset Station, 1301 W Sunset Rd ☎702/547-7777. Breakfast $6, lunch $7, dinner Sun–Thurs $9, Fri & Sat $13. All the Stations casinos offer similarly appealing, good-value buffets, and attract large crowds of loyal locals. *Feast Around The World*, in the very center of Sunset Station, is emblematic of the bunch, featuring a wide range of international cuisines dispensed by sections like "Mama Mia's" pizzas, "Chinatown," "Country Bar B Que," and "Viva Mexico." Friday and Saturday are steak nights, hence the higher prices.

Firelight Buffet

Sam's Town, 5111 Boulder Hwy ☎702/454-8044. Lunch Mon–Fri only $7; dinner Sat–Mon $11, Tues $10, Wed $13, Thurs & Fri $17. Now that it has been overhauled to keep up with the city's latest trends – most notably the craze for "action cooking," where chefs prepare food in front of you – the buffet at Sam's Town ranks among the best of the "locals" options. Dinner prices vary due to the specialties: Tuesday is Italian, Wednesday is steak, and Thursday and Friday see a seafood extravaganza, when selections include steamed crab, raw and cooked oysters, shrimp, and Cajun fish dishes.

Bars and lounges

Crown and Anchor

1350 E Tropicana Ave ☎702/739-8676, ⓦwww.crownandanchorlv.com. Daily 24hr. Counterfeit English pub in the University District, with mock-Tudor decor and an often raucous frat-boy atmosphere. Lots of European beers on draft (Newcastle, Stella, Tetley's, and such), plus a pool table, quiz nights, and English soccer games on the TV.

Double Down Saloon

4640 Paradise Rd ☎702/791-5775, ⓦwww.doubledownsaloon.com. Daily 24hr. Cool, dark, post-apocalyptic bar on the edge of the University District, furnished from thrift stores and daubed with psychedelic scrawlings. When obscure live bands aren't playing, the fabulously eclectic jukebox surely is.

Freezone

610 E Naples Drive ☎702/794-2300, ⓦwww.freezonelv.com. Daily 24hr. Busy gay-district bar, popular with women and men alike, two blocks south of the Hard Rock. Besides the drag acts (10pm Fri and Sat), it also features an all-male revue every Thursday, while its restaurant serves good food daily 6pm–2am.

Gaudí Bar

Sunset Station, 1301 W Sunset Rd, Henderson ☎702/547-7777. Daily 24hr. By far the weirdest and most wonderful casino lounge in Las Vegas. Sunset Station claims to "have left no tile unbroken" to create this billowing mosaic-encrusted toadstool of a tribute to sublimely surreal Spanish architect Gaudí, complete with faux-sky underbelly and best appreciated with the aid of a $4 specialty martini.

Goodtimes Bar & Grill

1775 E Tropicana Ave ☎702/736-9494. Daily 24hr. Welcoming neighborhood gay bar in the same mini-mall as the Liberace Museum. With happy hours from both 5am to 7am and 5pm to 7pm on Tuesday, Thursday & Sunday, it's usually a quiet, friendly place to hang out, though there's a hectic beer bust on Monday from 11pm–3am.

Gordon Biersch Brewery

3987 Paradise Rd ☎702/312-5247, ⓦwww.gordonbiersch.com/restaurants. Mon & Sun 11.30am–midnight, Tues–Sat 11.30am–2am. Cavernous and ultra-trendy chain microbrewery a mile off the Strip, packed with local big spenders (including *a lot* of singles) and featuring fine lagers brewed on-site, decent food, and live music from swing to reggae. Perhaps its best feature, though, is one that veteran Vegas bar-hoppers can appreciate: no slot machines.

Las Vegas Eagle

3430 E Tropicana Ave ☎702/458-8662. Daily 24hr. Dimly-lit, male-dominated Levi's-and-leathers gay bar, roughly four miles east of the Strip, which has a small dance floor and a pool table, and hosts underwear nights every Wednesday, Friday & Saturday. Not a desperately beautiful joint, it attracts a primarily older crowd.

Quark's Bar

Star Trek Experience, Las Vegas Hilton, 3000 Paradise Rd ☎702/697-8725.

▼ LAS VEGAS EAGLE

Sun–Thurs 11am–10pm, Fri & Sat 11am–11pm. No self-respecting Trekkie will want to miss this fun, futuristic vision, modeled on the bar from the *Deep Space Nine* series. Besides Romulan Ale, you can order all manner of bizarre alien food and drink.

Spotlight Lounge

957 E Sahara Ave ☎702/696-0202, ⓦwww.spotlightlv.com. Daily 24hr. Large, unglamorous but very friendly gay bar in the Commercial Center. Happy hour on Monday 9pm–midnight, while Friday is leather night, with free pizza.

Clubs and music venues

The Beach

365 Convention Center Drive ☎702/731-1925, ⓦwww.beachlv.com. Daily 24hr; club after 10pm. Cover (men only) usually $10. This round-the-clock multi-room bar and dance club, opposite the Convention Center, is at heart a permanent Spring Break, attracting a very young crowd to the massive dance floor (decked out with palm trees and coconuts) downstairs, and sports bar upstairs. Sunday, Monday & Wednesday are "Ladies Nights," when ladies drink for free 10pm–midnight.

The Buffalo

4640 Paradise Rd ☎702/733-8355. Daily 24hr. Lively Levi's-and-leathers club in the heart of the city's gay district that's the headquarters for local gay motorcycle clubs. Beer busts, especially Friday nights and Sunday afternoons, are a bigger deal than music or dancing.

Gipsy

4605 Paradise Rd ☎702/731-1919. Daily 10pm–6am. No cover before midnight; usually $5 later. High-profile gay dance club, where apart from the free cruise nights on Wednesdays, there's normally some form of live entertainment to justify the cover charge. Go-go boys perform Friday 11.30pm. The elaborate decor attracts young ingenues and local celebs.

The Joint

Hard Rock Hotel, 4455 Paradise Rd ☎702/693-5066. The Hard Rock's 1400-person showroom remains the Vegas venue of choice for big-name touring rock acts, not least because its affluent baby-boomer clientele enables bands like Aerosmith to charge $180 for a ticket. Ticket prices for performers as diverse as Elvis Costello, Social Distortion, Sonic Youth, and Neil Young range roughly between $40 and $80; the cheaper rates are for the much less atmospheric balcony, and "standing-room" tickets with poor views.

▼ THE JOINT

▲ THE RAILHEAD

The Railhead

Boulder Station, 4111 Boulder Hwy ⊤702/432-7777. Daily 24hr. Cover typically $20 on weekends. Set in an ordinary locals casino, the *Railhead* is a sizable and appealing lounge, where the big stage welcomes not only country names like Merle Haggard and Jerry Lee Lewis, but also soul, R&B, and reggae acts.

Whiskey Bar

Green Valley Ranch, 2300 Paseo Verde Parkway, Henderson ⊤702/617-7560, ⑩www.midnightoilbars.com. Daily 4pm–4am. No cover. Run by Rande Gerber, Cindy Crawford's husband, the ultra-chic *Whiskey Bar*, overlooking the Green Valley's pool, has an irresistible retro feel. Only VIPs get to enjoy the "opium dens," which come complete with plush sofas and TVs, but its big-name DJs and relatively laid-back atmosphere are readily accessible to all.

Shops

Albion Book Company

2466 E Desert Inn Rd ⊤702/792-9554. Daily 10am–6pm. Albion has Las Vegas's best stock of secondhand books, with over 150,000 titles, plus a big collection of used audio books at bargain prices.

Big B's

4761 S Maryland Parkway ⊤702/732-4433, ⑩www.bigbsmusic.com.

Mon–Sat 11am–9pm, Sun noon–6pm. University District music store, with well-informed staff and a large stock of CDs and DVDs, both new and used; some great prices on box sets, as well.

The Boulevard

3528 S Maryland Parkway at Desert Inn Blvd ⊤702/732-8949, ⑩www .blvdmall.com. Mon–Sat 10am–9pm, Sun 11am–6pm. This large single-story shopping mall totally lacks the glamour of its Strip counterparts, but it's the locals' favorite for day-to-day shopping. Anchored by department stores like Sears, JC Penney, Dillard's, and Macy's, it holds over 150 outlets, including Gap, Victoria's Secret, Body Shop, Radio Shack, and the entire gamut of Foot-lockers, plus a good food court.

Buffalo Exchange

4110 S Maryland Parkway ⊤702/791-3960, ⑩www.buffaloexchange.com. Mon–Sat 11am–7pm, Sun noon–6pm. Although less characterful than the Attic (see p.122), this Western chain of vintage-clothing stores is ultimately a more dependable source of inexpensive retro items, especially shoes.

Galleria at Sunset

1300 W Sunset Rd, Henderson ⊤702/434-0202, ⑩www .galleriaatsunset.com. Mon–Sat 10am–9pm, Sun 11am–6pm. This mall (anchored by Dillard's and JC Penney, and featuring many of the usual chain suspects in between) is slightly smaller than the older Boulevard, but it stands at the heart of a busy shopping district – eight miles southeast of the Strip, opposite Sunset Station – with neighbors including a Borders and a Barnes & Noble.

Day trips

Spend more than a day or two in Las Vegas's casinos, and you'll soon be gasping for a blast of sunlight and fresh air. Fortunately, there are some exhilarating day-trip destinations close by. The most obvious targets lie to the west in the Spring Mountains, where monumental walls cradle the desert fastness of Red Rock Canyon. To the north, wooded slopes rise toward the summit of Mount Charleston, and further to the northeast is the incandescent moonscape of the Valley of Fire. While neither Hoover Dam nor Lake Mead counts as a natural wonder, each is still every bit as breathtaking. As it's a 600-mile round-trip drive to the Grand Canyon, we've only covered tours that can get you there and back in a day.

Red Rock Canyon

20 miles west of Las Vegas on Hwy-159/Charleston Rd ☎702/363-1921, ⓦwww.redrockcanyon.blm.gov. The sheer 3000-foot escarpment that towers above Red Rock Canyon National Conservation Area – the closest concentration of classic Southwestern canyon scenery to the city – is clearly visible from hotel windows along the Strip, with every fiery detail picked out each morning by the rising sun. What you can't see until you enter the park is the cactus-strewn desert basin set deep into those mighty walls, surrounded by stark red cliffs pierced repeatedly by narrow canyons accessible only on foot.

Run by the Federal Bureau of Land Management, Red Rock Canyon covers almost 200,000 acres of wilderness, and like other BLM areas, is less groomed for tourists than national parks or monuments. Thus, while there's over thirty miles of hiking trails, they're not as well signed or maintained as you might expect, and it's all too easy for novice walkers to get lost.

Red Rock Canyon's smart **visitor center** (daily 8am–4.30pm) is located to the left of Hwy-159, shortly after it veers south to follow Red Rock Wash, at the start of the Scenic Drive. Inside, displays and

---

Red Rock Canyon hiking practicalities

While Red Rock Canyon is great for hiking – and camping, call ☎702/515-5050 for permits – there are a number of things to keep in mind. The canyon is subject to "leave no trace" rules, meaning you should minimize your contact with wildlife, stay on established trails, and pack out everything you bring in. Since temperatures can soar above 105°F/41°C, bring plenty of water. Be warned also that the desert is home to mountain lions and rattlesnakes. For more detailed information on Red Rock Canyon hiking, go to ⓦwww.redrockcanyonlv.org.

▲ RED ROCK CANYON

models explain the geological formation and wildlife of the canyon. If you plan to hike, buy a good map here before you set off; the free handouts aren't up to the job. Outside is a landscaped terrace commanding a panoramic view of the canyon's main features, facing into a natural amphitheater of Aztec sandstone that soars on three sides of the central basin. In the foreground, small gardens are planted with various cactus species, including cholla and Joshua trees, and an enclosure of rare desert tortoises holds the canyon's "spokes-tortoise," Mojave Max. Paving stones along the Dedication Walkway here are engraved with memorials to the victims of September 11, 2001. Farther back, the Wilson Cliffs to the left are topped by a layer of gray limestone, which has preserved them from erosion and left them taller than the rounded Calico Hills to the right.

A one-way loop road beyond the visitor center, the **Scenic Drive** (daily 6am–dusk; $5 per vehicle, bicycles free) meanders for thirteen miles around the edge of Red Rock Canyon before rejoining the main highway a couple of miles southwest of the visitor center.

Designed for drivers (not pedestrians), it's also popular with cyclists, who can bike on designated trails as well as on the road itself. Overlooks along the way serve as trailheads for hikes of varying lengths.

The most dramatic views on the Scenic Drive come early, as you head straight toward the Calico Hills that form the basin's northeastern wall. From two successive overlooks, **Calico Vistas 1 and 2**, it's possible to scramble short distances down from the road and into the hills to find yourself dwarfed amid these crumbling domes of cream and red sandstone.

Further along, the **Calico Tanks Trail** (2.5 miles round-trip) heads up from Sandstone Quarry and beyond the visible rim to reach the largest of the area's natural "tanks." The rainwater collected and stored in these depressions was once a valuable resource for nomadic desert peoples.

The canyon's easiest route, the **Red Rock Canyon Discovery Trail** starts at Willow Spring, a short way up a spur road seven miles along the Scenic Drive. The 1.5-mile trail follows the tree-filled minor canyon formed by Lost Creek, passing rock shelters used by the region's prehistoric inhabitants.

More energetic hikers will prefer the **Pine Creek Canyon Trail** (5 miles round-trip). From the trailhead – just under eleven miles from the visitor center – to the ponderosas marking Pine Creek, it takes around twenty minutes, following a sandy red footpath fringed with cacti. The main trail continues up to the right to a red-capped monolith dividing two forked canyons.

Mount Charleston

30 miles northwest of Las Vegas, US-95 then west on Hwy-157/Kyle Canyon Rd. Las Vegas residents desperate to escape the summer heat flock to the Spring Mountain Recreation Area. Forming part of the Toiyabe National Forest, it's more widely known as Mount Charleston, on account of its highest point, the 11,918-foot Charleston Peak. Ten thousand years ago, the isolated Spring Mountains formed a natural refuge for wildlife from the lakes that filled the Las Vegas valley, and it retained its own unique ecosystem as the rest of the region dried out. In fact, many of its plants and animals, including one unique species of chipmunk, are found nowhere else on earth. The cool wooded slopes of Mount Charleston offer some great hiking, and in winter you can even drive out for a day of skiing or snowboarding at Lee Canyon. Higher elevations usually remain covered by snow between mid-October and mid-May each year, while the streams and waterfalls only carry substantial flows during the thaw in spring and early summer.

Driving into the Spring Mountains on Hwy-157, the road at first remains relatively level, as the hills rise on either side. The ascent is so gradual that it's only when your ears pop that you realize you've left the valley behind. As the closest part of the mountains to Las Vegas, **Kyle Canyon** is the main day-trip destination from the city, and its popularity shows, as with each passing year, a few more buildings appear on its slopes. Still, there's nowhere up here to buy gas or basic groceries, so stock up accordingly beforehand.

Seventeen miles up from US-95, beyond the *Mount Charleston Hotel*, your surroundings change from yuccas and cacti into forests of pine, fir, and mahogany. Half a mile past the Hwy-158 turnoff stands the **Kyle Guard and Information Station** (Mon & Thurs–Sun 9am–4pm; ☎702/872-5486), where rangers can supply trail guides and up-to-date weather forecasts.

A mile up Hwy-157, past the station, a short spur road climbs straight on up for a few hundred yards, to the trailhead for the **Mary Jane Falls Trail** (2.5 miles round-trip). This

▼ MOUNT CHARLESTON

▲ LAKE MEAD MARINA

hike follows a disused road for about a mile, before ascending a series of exhausting switchbacks to the twin Mary Jane Falls at the head of the canyon. Fed by separate springs, the falls are at their strongest in early summer, but that's not a good time to enter the caves immediately behind them, which remain icy until later in the year.

Half a mile further along Hwy-157, shortly before it dead-ends at *Mount Charleston Lodge*, the **Cathedral Rock Trail** (3 miles round-trip) sets off from a roadside parking lot. Starting at 7600ft and climbing a further thousand feet along a rough but not very steep footpath, the trek can be pretty grueling for anyone unused to such elevations. At the top of the promontory known as Cathedral Rock, you're rewarded with views all the way back down Kyle Canyon, as well as onward to the smooth, bald dome of Charleston Peak, sticking out above the treeline.

Off Hwy-158, not far short of Lee Canyon, the clearly signed **Desert View Trail** is a short, paved footpath with an unlikely history. On eight separate days in 1957, vast crowds assembled up here to watch the explosions from atomic bomb testing.

These days, you have to settle simply for a vast desert panorama, which doesn't extend as far as Las Vegas itself.

The most scenic stretch of road in the Spring Mountains has to be **Hwy-158**, which runs north from Hwy-157 for nine miles across the face of the mountains to connect Kyle Canyon with Lee Canyon and Hwy-156. Pullouts along the way provide opportunities to survey the desert far below and you may even spot caves said to have once housed bandits preying on travelers using the old Mormon Trail across the valley.

From the north end of Hwy-158, Hwy-156 runs three miles southwest into the heart of **Lee Canyon**, where the trees have been cut back to create southern Nevada's only ski area, the tiny Las Vegas Ski and Snowboard Resort.

Lake Mead

30 miles southeast from Las Vegas, Hwy-582/Boulder Hwy to US-93.
The single most popular day trip from Las Vegas is to the vast artificial Lake Mead and to the mighty Hoover Dam that created it. As for the lake, it makes a bizarre spectacle, utterly unnatural yet undeniably

▲ ALAN BIBLE VISITOR CENTER

impressive, with its bright blue waters a vivid counterpoint to the surrounding desert. Both the lake and its 550-mile shoreline, however, can be excruciatingly crowded year-round.

On a stark sandstone slope beside US-93, four miles north-east of Boulder City, the **Alan Bible Visitor Center** (daily 8.30am–4.30pm; ☎702/293-8990, ⓦwww.nps.gov/lame) is the main source of informa-tion on Lake Mead National Recreation Area. Even if you don't need details of how to sail, scuba-dive, water-ski, or fish from the lake's seven separate marinas, it's worth calling in to enjoy a sweeping prospect of the whole thing. Pick up some safety advice, too – the lake averages three fatal water acci-dents per month.

Though Lake Mead straddles the border between Nevada and Arizona, the best views come from the Nevada side. From the visitor center, Hwy-166, better known as **Lakeshore Scenic Drive**, follows the lake's western shore as far as Las Vegas Bay,

with spur roads leading down to Lake Mead Marina (☎702/293-3484, ⓦwww.sevencrown.com) and Las Vegas Boat Harbor (☎702/293-1191, ⓦwww .boatinglakemead.com). As well as boat and jet-ski rental, both marinas offer restaurants and stores, but they're functional rather than pleasant places to stop. In between the two, Lake Mead Cruises Landing (☎702/293-6180, ⓦwww.lake-meadcruises.com) is the base of operations for the *Desert Princess*, an imitation paddlewheeler that makes two to four excursions daily, calling at Hoover Dam. Prices range from $20 for a morning cruise to $54 for a Sat-urday-night dinner and dance.

Hoover Dam

33 miles southeast from Las Vegas, Hwy-582/Boulder Hwy to US-93. Designed to block the Colorado River and supply low-cost water and electricity to the cities of the Southwest, the 726-foot-high Hoover Dam is among the tallest dams ever built, and at 660ft across at the base, it's

nearly as wide as it is tall. It was completed in 1935, as the first step in the Bureau of Reclamation program that culminated in the Glen Canyon Dam at the far end of the Grand Canyon, and the creation of Lake Powell. In addition to creating Lake Mead, Hoover Dam is likely responsible for modern Las Vegas's very existence, not so much as a source of energy – only four percent of Las Vegas's electricity comes from hydroelectric power – but because the workers who built it triggered the city's first gambling-fueled boom.

Visits to Hoover Dam have been restricted since the 9/11 attacks convinced the authorities that it was a potential terrorist target. In addition, while private vehicles are unaffected, commercial traffic is no longer permitted to cross the dam. If you're happy to get just a general view of the scale of the thing, drive across the top of the dam into Arizona, and squeeze into one of the parking lots on the far side. But for a good close-up view, pay $5 to get into the huge parking lot on the Nevada side of the river (daily 8am–6pm). From here you can walk down to the dam itself and stroll along the top of it, looking towards Lake Mead from one sidewalk and then peering down the awesome drop to the river from the other. A splendid Deco monument on the Nevada side commemorates the dam's opening by Franklin Roosevelt in 1935. At the nearby **Hoover Dam Visitor Center** (daily: April–Sept 8.30am–5.45pm; Oct–March 9.15am–4.15pm; ☎293-1824, ⓦwww.usbr.gov/lc/hooverdam; $10) you can inspect displays on the dam's history and construction, and join a "Discovery Tour," taking an elevator ride down to see the giant turbine room at the bottom. However, as the former "hard-hat" tours, which allowed visitors to step out into the open air down at the base of the dam, have been discontinued, the admission price may seem a bit steep.

▲ HOOVER DAM

Valley Of Fire

50 miles northeast of Las Vegas, I-15 to Hwy-169. While Red Rock Canyon certainly makes a tasty appetizer, to experience the true scale and splendor of the Southwestern deserts, a trip to the Valley of Fire is necessary. Its multicolored, strangely eroded rocks are the solidified remains of sand dunes laid down at the time of the dinosaurs, 150 million years ago. If they seem familiar, you may have seen them in any number of movies and TV shows, from *One Million Years BC* to *Star Trek – The Next Generation*.

Hwy-169 cuts away east from I-15, cresting the aptly named Muddy Mountains to enter **Valley of Fire State Park** (Ⓦ www.parks.nv.gov/vf.htm; $6 per-vehicle entrance fee). A huge panorama opens up ahead, stretching down toward Lake Mead, but the road has to pick its way gingerly down, threading between abrupt, jagged out-crops. After passing the entrance station, you soon come to the first of the big red rocks, the ridged, bulbous Beehives.

A little further on, a 5.5-mile spur road past the park's **visitor center** (daily 8.30am–4.30pm; ☎702/397-2088) leads through a wonderland of misshapen stone monstrosities, worn smooth by millennia of wind and rain and striped in a broad palate of colors. Cream, yellow, gold, pink, and purple strata are interspersed among the lurid, omnipresent red. Many hikers set off walking when the road dead-ends at the White Domes, but that entails plowing through thick sand drifts, and there's a better trail earlier on. The enjoyable and easy **Mouse's Tank trail** (1 mile round-trip) starts less than a mile north of the visitor center and follows a sandy wash through Petroglyph Canyon. The trail stops when the ground suddenly drops away at the far end of the canyon, where run-off after desert storms has cut deep channels into the rock. Scrambling up the slopes adjacent to the edge

▼ HIKING IN THE VALLEY OF FIRE

▲ RED SANDSTONE ROCKS, VALLEY OF FIRE

enables you to peer down into Mouse's Tank, a natural reservoir that was the hideout of Mouse, a fugitive Paiute Indian, during the 1890s.

Alongside Hwy-169, about three miles east of the visitor center, is **Elephant Rock**, one of the most photographed features of the Valley of Fire. Reached via a short but steep trail from the parking lot at the park's east entrance, it does indeed bear an amazing resemblance to a petrified pachyderm, dipping its trunk into the hillside.

A mile east outside the Valley of Fire State Park, Hwy-169 meets Hwy-167, **Northshore Drive**, which circles back south toward Las Vegas, a fifty-mile drive that takes you through some utterly stunning wilderness. Desolate and forbidding sandstone mountains soar in your path, the road dwindling to a thin gray streak dwarfed beneath stark serrated cliffs. Its name, however, referring to its position by Lake Mead, is mis-

leading – you almost never see the lake itself, which remains on the far side of a high ridge.

The Lost City Museum

Hwy-169, Overton ☎702/397-2193, ⓦwww.comnett.net/~kolson. Daily 8.30am–4.30pm. $2. Overton's intriguing Lost City Museum preserves the largest Nevada settlement of the Ancestral Puebloans, who inhabited the Colorado Plateau between around 300 BC and 1150 AD. The so-called "Lost City" was in fact more of an elongated village. Stretching for around thirty miles along the Moapa Valley, and originally known to archeologists as the Pueblo Grande de Nevada, its ruins were partly submerged by the creation of Lake Mead in the 1930s. At that time, the finest artifacts from the site were gathered into this museum, which was given a catchy name in the hope of making it easier to raise funds.

Displays at the museum are still very much rooted in the

▲ GRAND CANYON

1930s – techniques like painting over a slab of genuine petro-glyphs would appall modern archeologists – but there's still plenty to fascinate casual visitors. The whole structure is designed in a mock-Pueblo style, with a replica of a dig on a genuine site inside, and there are reconstructions of Pueblo buildings, also on their original sites, in the garden outside.

The Grand Canyon

Whatever impression Las Vegas tour companies may give you, the Grand Canyon is nowhere near the city. The canyon's South Rim – the headquarters of the national park, the center for tourist activity, and where all those stunning photos are taken – is 290 miles from Las Vegas by road, while the quieter but equally impressive

Grand Canyon tours

It is just possible, if not especially recommended, to take a **bus** to the South Rim and back in a day; Grayline (☎702/384-1234, ⊛www.grayline.com) does a fourteen-hour round-trip for $150, and also a nine-hour trip to the West Rim for $140, while the Missing Link Tours (☎800/209-8586, ⊛www .tmltours.com) visits the West Rim for $119, with overnight camping trips $189.

The variety of Grand Canyon **aerial tours** – a much more practical, if more expensive, way to do the trip – on offer is endless. All include an aerial view of Hoover Dam, which lies conveniently en route, as well as a shuttle service to and from your hotel, and cost roughly $100–500. Look for advertisements in free local magazines that feature two-for-one deals, or check the operators' websites for specials.

Air Vegas Airlines ☎702/736-3599 or 800/255-7474, ⊛www.airvegas .com. Helicopter tours of the West Rim from $229, or an eight-hour trip to the South Rim, including a bus tour, for $250.

Heli USA ☎702/736-8787 or 800/359-8727, ⊛www.heliusa.com. Helicopter flights from Las Vegas to a remote West Rim ranch, where you can go horse riding or stay the night in a log cabin. Prices start from around $300.

Papillon Helicopters ☎702/736-7243 or 888/635-7272, ⊛www.papillon .com. A huge range of helicopter tours, including landing beside the river at the West Rim for $349, and either riding in a bus ($245) or a fixed-wing plane ($329) to the South Rim and taking a helicopter tour there.

Scenic Airlines ☎702/638-3200 or 800/634-6801, ⊛www.scenic.com. Fixed-wing air tours, including West Rim without a landing for $109, or landing at the South Rim for $224, with an optional bus tour for another $20.

PLACES Day trips

North Rim is only a little closer, along a far less traveled route. Instead, most bus and helicopter tours advertised as visiting the canyon from Las Vegas actually take you only about 130 miles to the so-called West Rim, a Colorado River overlook on the Hualapai Indian Reservation. Although this is a dramatic and isolated desert viewpoint in its own right, it's simply not on the same scale as the real thing.

Accommodation

Hotels

Las Vegas is the hotel capital of the planet, holding fourteen of the world's twenty largest hotels, and all of the US top ten. Almost all of Vegas's 135,000 rooms are in hotels attached to large casinos, with the vast majority in the giant properties lined up along the Strip, where at least fifteen casinos boast more than three thousand rooms apiece.

Where you stay makes a huge difference. It can take half an hour to walk to the Strip from a room in the *MGM Grand* or *Caesars Palace*, so choose a hotel where you'll be happy to spend time. The most convenient locations are unquestionably the southern end of the Strip, around Tropicana Avenue, and the Central Strip area near Flamingo Avenue. Downtown hotels are usually much less glamorous, while those located well off the Strip can be OK but are only worth considering if you don't mind driving.

Whatever you may have heard, Las Vegas hotels no longer offer incredibly cheap deals, though prices are roughly thirty percent lower than you might pay for similar accommodation in other US cities. It's true that serious gamblers can get free accommodation, but you have first to establish a track record of gambling thousands of dollars – a strange definition of "free."

Hotel rooms in Las Vegas tend to be much the same as in any generic American chain, with most casinos making only token efforts to match rooms to their overall "themes."

No conventional motels now survive on the Strip, though plenty are scattered elsewhere in the city. Since rates at these places tend to be no great savings, the reviews below concentrate on accommodation at the major Strip and downtown casinos – each of which is described in detail in earlier chapters – with just a few exceptional properties and budget options elsewhere.

Reservations and prices

Besides the usual travel websites, when looking for a hotel room you can try the **Las Vegas Convention & Visitors Authority**, which offers an availability and reservations service (☎877/847-4858). You can also try the **Las Vegas Hotel Reservation Center** (☎702/873-8041 or 800/394-7750, ⊛www .lasvegashotel.com).

Precise **room rates** vary widely; stay in the same room for a week, and you'll likely pay a different rate each night. You may find discounts online, or simply by saying you're attending a convention, or that you belong to the AAA or the British AA. However, the only surefire way to get a cut-price room is to visit during the week rather than the weekend. Rates everywhere rise enormously on Friday or Saturday, $100 or more extra per night in the big-name casinos. Many hotels only take reservations covering Friday and Saturday, and won't accept Saturday arrivals.

Hotel rates in this chapter refer to the approximate cost of a double room throughout most of the year. Note that all rates shown are subject to an additional room tax, nine percent on the Strip, and eleven percent downtown.

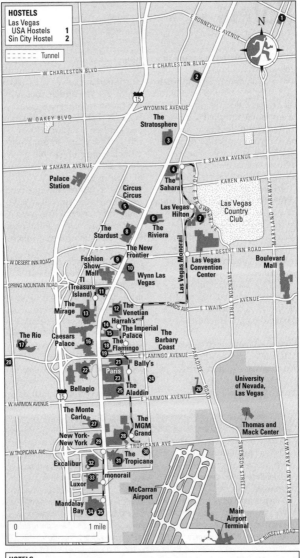

The Strip

Aladdin Resort and Casino 3667 Las Vegas Blvd S ☎702/785-5555 or 877/333-9474, ⊛www.aladdincasino .com. As described on p.71, the financially troubled *Aladdin* is due to be reincarnated as *Planet Hollywood* in 2006. Hopefully this won't result in any major changes besides name and decoration, because it's always been one of the Strip's nicer and most reasonably priced places to stay. *Aladdin* is much more manageable in size than most of its giant neighbors, with each of its 2600 rooms lying within easy reach of an elevator, and no need to drag your bags through the casino when you check in. While falling just short of the very highest category of luxury, and lacking any particular theming, the rooms are spacious, with separate bath and shower. The on-site dining and shopping are first class, and there's a good pool and a great spa. Sun–Thurs $99, Fri & Sat $149.

Bally's Las Vegas 3645 Las Vegas Blvd S ☎702/739-4111 or 800/722-5597, ⊛www.ballyslv.com. Once the world's largest hotel (as the first *MGM Grand*), *Bally's* is now overshadowed and outclassed by neighbors like *Bellagio*, across the Strip, and its own next-door sister property, *Paris*. While the casino itself is quite dull, the large refurbished rooms are pretty good, and with *Bally's* being on the Monorail it makes a convenient, if not exciting, place to stay. Sun–Thurs $74, Fri & Sat $119.

The Barbary Coast Hotel & Casino 3595 Las Vegas Blvd S ☎702/737-7111 or 888/227-2279, ⊛www .barbarycoastcasino.com. The smallest of the Strip casinos is a real throwback, offering a mere 200 chintzy guestrooms decked out to recall the San Francisco of a century ago. Once you get away from the gloomy public areas, though, it's all quite cozy, and the rooms are heavily oversubscribed at weekends. Sun–Thurs $59, Fri & Sat $99.

Bellagio Resort & Casino 3600 Las Vegas Blvd S ☎702/693-7111 or 888/987-6667, ⊛www.bellagio.com.

Bellagio represents the very top end of the Vegas spectrum, a fact reflected in its rates. Rooms are extremely luxurious, with plush European furnishings and marble bathrooms; the pool complex is superb; and the restaurants are among the very best in town. By world standards, it's excellent value, but you can live the high life in other Vegas casinos – less tasteful perhaps, but much more fun – for half the price. Sun–Thurs $169, Fri & Sat $279.

Caesars Palace 3570 Las Vegas Blvd S ☎702/731-7222 or 800/634-6661, ⊛www.caesarspalace.com. Despite having epitomized Las Vegas luxury ever since the 1960s, *Caesars Palace* has only recently begun to match its neighbors in terms of numbers of rooms, with yet more expansion in the pipeline. The older rooms still burst with pseudo-Roman splendor – think ornate columns, and classical sculptures displayed in wall niches – while those in the newer Tower are more conventionally elegant. Standard rates aren't low, but paying as little as $10 extra can get you a suite with a four-poster bed and mirrored ceiling. Although its colossal size can make this a baffling labyrinth to negotiate, the top-class attractions, pools, restaurants, and fantastic shopping at the Forum, ranks *Caesars* among the best bets in town. Sun–Thurs $119, Fri & Sat $199.

Circus Circus Hotel/Casino 2880 Las Vegas Blvd S ☎702/734-0410 or 800/444-2472, ⊛www.circuscircus .com. Only *Excalibur* matches *Circus Circus* for its family appeal and ambience, and both are similarly popular with budget tour groups. Kids love the theme park and (almost) nonstop circus acts, adults love the low room rates. Being able to park outside your door in the motel-like Manor section at the back is a real plus, but the rooms themselves are pretty grim; it's worth paying a little more to stay in one of the Towers instead. Sun–Thurs $49, Fri & Sat $79.

Excalibur Hotel & Casino 3850 Las Vegas Blvd S ☎702/597-7700 or 800/937-7777, ⊛www.excaliburcasino .com. This fantastically garish fake castle offers plenty to amuse the kids while the adults gamble away their college funds, but even ongoing redecoration has failed to make its 4000 rooms anything special. Few rooms have views to speak of – many face in rather than out – their theming is minimal, and there are no baths, only showers. Thanks to an endless stream of tour groups and families, the whole place tends to be uncomfortably crowded; expect long lines at the restaurants. Sun–Thurs $59, Fri & Sat $99.

The Flamingo 3555 Las Vegas Blvd S ☎702/733-3111 or 800/732-2111, ⊛www.flamingolasvegas.com. Bugsy Siegel's oft-renovated *Flamingo* may not be in the top rank of Vegas casinos, but it's a solid B-list choice, with a very central location, 4000 well-appointed rooms, and a great tropical-themed pool complex, complete with genuine flamingos. Sun–Thurs $79, Fri & Sat $129.

Four Seasons Hotel Las Vegas 3960 Las Vegas Blvd S ☎702/632-5000, ⊛www.fourseasons.com/lasvegas/. The first Las Vegas venture of the very upmarket *Four Seasons* hotel chain exists in a strange symbiotic relationship with the *Mandalay Bay*. Although it seems like an entirely separate building, entered via its own driveway from the Strip, that section only houses the lobby and restaurants; the 424 extravagantly opulent guestrooms are in fact on the 35th to 39th floors of the *Mandalay Bay*. The hotel's unique selling point is as a luxurious refuge from the noise and pace of the Strip – you can come and go without ever seeing a slot machine, let alone contending with the usual crowds. There's also a gorgeous pool. Sun–Thurs $199, Fri & Sat $319.

Harrah's Las Vegas 3475 Las Vegas Blvd S ☎702/369-5000 or 800/392-9002, ⊛www.harrahsvegas.com. *Harrah's* addition of a 35-story tower, on a great site facing *Caesars Palace*, means that it now offers a total of 2700 bright, big, but somewhat anonymous and not exceptionally cheap rooms. Expect improvements soon, to suit *Harrah's* status as the flagship location for one of Las Vegas's very major players. Sun–Thurs $79, Fri & Sat $139.

The Imperial Palace 3535 Las Vegas Blvd S ☎702/731-3311 or 800/634-6441, ⊛www.imperialpalace.com. Behind its hideous mock-pagoda facade, the *Imperial Palace* is, for travelers happy to forego Las Vegas luxury, one of the best-value options in the heart of the Strip. Its standard rooms are adequate if not exciting – all have balconies, though, which is quite rare – while the irresistibly bizarre "luv tub" suites, at about $30 extra, offer huge beds, even bigger sunken baths, and mirrors everywhere you can imagine. Sun–Thurs $59, Fri & Sat $99.

Luxor Las Vegas 3900 Las Vegas Blvd S ☎702/262-4102 or 888/777-0188, ⊛www.luxor.com. Spending a night or two in this vast smoked-glass pyramid is one of the great Las Vegas experiences; any longer than that, and you may well be sick of the endless trek to reach your room from the nearest "inclinator" (elevator in *Luxor*-speak). All the 2000 rooms in the pyramid itself face outwards, with tremendous views, and they're much larger than usual – partly to minimize the effect of the slanting windows, partly because there's space for them to stretch into the hollow interior. Unlike the additional 2000 rooms in the newer tower next door, however – some of which have jacuzzis next to the windows – most pyramid rooms have showers only, not baths. All are enjoyably Egyptian-themed, with Art Deco furnishings and Pharaonic bedspreads. Sun–Thurs $79, Fri & Sat $119.

Mandalay Bay Resort & Casino 3950 Las Vegas Blvd S ☎702/632-7777 or 888/632-7000, also 877/632-7700 for THEhotel, ⊛www.mandalaybay.com. *Mandalay Bay*, an upscale young-adult playground that tries (pretty successfully) to beat the *Hard Rock* at its own game, can feel a little far removed from the bustle of the central Strip. Each of its luxurious rooms has a superb bath and walk-in shower; the vaguely Asiatic theming varies, and the floor plans can be a bit odd, but some have great Strip views. A second 43-story tower houses the nominally distinct *THEhotel*, which has its own lobby to enable guests to avoid the casino area altogether, and holds around 1100 extremely stylish and expensive suites. *Mandalay Bay* Sun–Thurs $129, Fri & Sat $179; *THEhotel* Sun–Thurs $189, Fri & Sat $299.

The MGM Grand Hotel/Casino 3799 Las Vegas Blvd S ☏702/891-1111 or 800/929-1111, ✆www.mgmgrand .com. The downsides of staying at Vegas's largest hotel, with 5000 rooms currently available and more on the way, are that any kind of service, especially check-in, can take a horrendously long time, as can just walking from one end of the place to the other. There are plenty of plusses, however, including the standard of accommodation you get for the price, and the presence of several of Las Vegas's finest restaurants. Guestrooms have a fun 1930s Hollywood feel, adorned with stills from MGM classics like *Gone With the Wind* or *Casablanca*, and all feature marble bathrooms. Sun–Thurs $89, Fri & Sat $139.

The Mirage 3400 Las Vegas Blvd S ☏702/791-7111 or 800/627-6667, ✆www.mirage.com. The glitzy *Mirage* is not the market leader it used to be, and its smallish rooms are complemented by even smaller bathrooms. Even so, the public areas downstairs remain impressive, the pool complex is nicely laid out, and the weekday rates for one of Las Vegas's most prestigious addresses aren't at all bad. Sun–Thurs $119, Fri & Sat $189.

The Monte Carlo Resort & Casino 3770 Las Vegas Blvd S ☏702/730-7000 or 800/311-8999, ✆www .monte-carlo.com. Despite having over 3000 rooms, the *Monte Carlo* maintains a lower profile than any similarly sized property along the Strip, cultivating a sedate, sophisticated image that attracts affluent older visitors rather than families. The location is good, in between *Bellagio* and *New York–New York*, while the huge pool area, complete with wave pool and rafting river, is a boon in summer. Sun–Thurs $89, Fri & Sat $129.

The New Frontier Hotel & Casino 3120 Las Vegas Blvd S ☏702/794-8200 or 800/634-6966, ✆www.frontierlv.com. The Strip's oldest resort has been refurbished many times, and may well have

vanished altogether by the time you read this. At time of writing, however, behind its rather tacky casino the hotel itself is spiffier than you might expect. The two-room suites in the newer Atrium Tower could even be called tasteful. Sun–Thurs $69, Fri & Sat $119.

New York–New York Hotel & Casino 3790 Las Vegas Blvd S ☏702/740-6050 or 800/693-6763, ✆www .nynyhotelcasino.com. Sheer attention to detail makes *New York–New York* the most enjoyable casino on the Strip. It's also small enough that guests don't have to spend half their visit shuffling down endless corridors. Although the elevators leave from lobbies designed to resemble specific Manhattan skyscrapers, once you get upstairs, the design is essentially the same from one part of the hotel to the other. However, the rooms are all very nice, if a bit small (like actual New York hotel rooms), and filled with Art Deco furnishings and flourishes, including nicely ornate closets, wardrobes, and headboards. Sun–Thurs $99, Fri & Sat $149.

Paris–Las Vegas 3655 Las Vegas Blvd S ☏702/946-7000 or 877/796-2096, ✆www.parislasvegas.com. The rooms and services at the flamboyant *Paris* don't attempt to match every luxury of Las Vegas's most upscale joints, and unlike the public spaces the ambience is basically generic American rather than French, but they're still pretty good quality for the price. For views, ambience, and central location – it's on the Monorail, as well – *Paris* more than holds its own. Sun–Thurs $129, Fri & Sat $179.

The Riviera Hotel & Casino 2901 Las Vegas Blvd S ☏702/734-5110 or 800/634-6753, ✆www.rivierahotel.com. Nothing about the longstanding *Riviera* casino makes it worth paying the comparatively inflated rates to stay in one of its 2000-plus very ordinary rooms. If you do, the newer Monaco Tower is marginally preferable to the older main building. Sun–Thurs $79, Fri & Sat $119.

The Sahara Hotel & Casino 2535 Las Vegas Blvd S ☏702/737-2111 or 888/696-2121, ✆www.saharavegas .com. The *Sahara*'s garish, quasi- (or queasy-) Moroccan rooms are in the finest Vegas tradition of overwrought decorating schemes, and they're reasonably priced, though the property itself is quite a trek north from the best parts of the Strip. Despite the presence of the roller coaster and NASCAR attractions, it caters more to older or business travelers rather than families with children. Sun–Thurs $59, Fri & Sat $79.

The Stardust Hotel & Casino 3000 Las Vegas Blvd S ☎702/732-6111 or 866/642-3120, ✉www.stardustlv.com. This Vegas veteran has seen better days, but the rooms in its new purple-tinted tower are attractive enough, even if they do loom intimidatingly close to its tiny pool. The two-story villas that line one side of the pool make a more appealing choice, not least because with their lesser amenities they work out significantly cheaper. Sun–Thurs $69, Fri & Sat $109.

The Stratosphere Hotel & Casino 2000 Las Vegas Blvd S ☎702/380-7777 or 800/998-6937, ✉www .stratospherehotel.com. The *Strato-sphere* has confounded the skeptics by surviving at all, despite its very unfashionable location at the far north end of the Strip, thanks largely to low room rates and a steady flow of budget tour groups. The 2500 rooms are large but still not fancy at all, and only have small windows, but the (hotel block) rooftop pool is pretty good. None of the accommodation is in the 100-story tower – rooms are located instead in a nondescript adjoining building – so don't expect amazing views, but if you can put up with the isolation it's not a bad deal, and more likely than most to have last-minute availability. Sun–Thurs $39, Fri & Sat $59.

TI 3300 Las Vegas Blvd S ☎702/894-7111 or 800/288-7206, ✉www .treasureisland.com. Formerly known as *Treasure Island*, this sister hotel to the neighboring *Mirage* (linked via a monorail) has distanced itself from its original family-centric orientation, and abandoned all the Jolly Roger theming. However, it's still a fun and wonderfully convenient place to stay, even if the rooms are small-ish and rather subdued

in a pastel-toned sort of way. Sun–Thurs $89, Fri & Sat $139.

The Tropicana Resort & Casino 3801 Las Vegas Blvd S ☎702/739-2222 or 888/826-8767, ✉www.tropicanalv.com. Faltering ever more obviously in its attempts to match its giant neighbors, and probably destined for the wrecker's ball before long, the *Tropicana* is no longer quite the delightful flower-filled oasis it set out to be in the late 1950s. The rooms are certainly showing their age, and come in three basic styles: French in the Paradise Tower, tropical in the Island Tower, or cramped but cheap in the old motel section at the back. At least the *Trop* still boasts the world's largest indoor-outdoor swimming pool, complete with swim-up gaming tables. Sun–Thurs $79, Fri & Sat $129.

The Venetian 3355 Las Vegas Blvd S ☎702/414-1000 or 877/883-6423, ✉www.venetian.com. This upscale behemoth has firmly established itself as the Strip's best-value luxury hotel; it maintains 98 percent occupancy year-round, so room rates remain resolutely inflexible. Even the standard rooms are split-level suites, with decadently comfortable antique-style canopied beds on a raised platform, plus roomy living rooms equipped with a fax machine/printer. Each also has a marble bath and walk-in shower. Within easy walking distance downstairs you'll find a mind-blowing array of shops and restaurants, while there's a big rooftop pool complex atop the main body of the hotel. The newer Venezia Tower offers even more opulence, plus (with its own check-in desk) a sense of being aloof from the casino bustle and typically costs from $40 per night extra. Sun–Thurs $199, Fri & Sat $279.

Wynn Las Vegas 3131 Las Vegas Blvd S ☎702/770-7100 or 877/770-7077, ✉www.wynnlasvegas.com. Although it had not opened at the time of writing, the accommodation here looked to be every bit as luxurious (and expensive) as at Wynn's previous property, *Bellagio*. There are some 2700 sizable rooms and suites, each with flat-screen TVs in both the living area and bathroom. If you're looking to really splurge, there are also villas overlooking the golf course, with massage rooms and private balconies. $250–450 (approximate).

Downtown Las Vegas

Binion's Horseshoe Hotel & Casino 128 E Fremont St ☎702/382-1600 or 800/622-6468, ⓦwww.binions.com. The hard-bitten gambler's hangout of choice offers a handful of no-frills rooms in the main building, and a couple of hundred marginally more appealing ones in what used to be the *Mint* next door. Sun–Thurs $29, Fri & Sat $49.

California Hotel & Casino 12 Ogden Ave ☎702/385-1222 or 800/634-6255 or 800/465-0711, ⓦwww.thecal.com. Most of the guests in this mid-range downtown casino are Hawaiian, thusly Hawaiian food and drink dominates the bars and restaurants. The actual rooms are plain but adequate. Sun–Thurs $49, Fri & Sat $69.

El Cortez Hotel & Casino 600 E Fremont St ☎702/385-5200 or 800/634-6703, ⓦwww.elcortezhotelcasino .com. Veteran downtown casino, located a couple of fairly dodgy blocks east of the Fremont Street Experience, where the cut-price rooms in the main building are a little better than the rather dismal gaming area downstairs might suggest. The mini-suites in the new tower are exceptional value, while the bargain-basement rooms in *Ogden House* across the street – private, en-suite, but utterly rudimentary – cost just $18. Hotel rooms Sun–Thurs $30, Fri & Sat $42.

Fitzgeralds Casino & Holiday Inn 301 E Fremont St ☎702/388-2400 or 800/274-5825, ⓦwww.fitzgeralds.com. Very central but generic downtown hotel, where the guestrooms feature standard-issue *Holiday Inn* decor rather than any locally flavored glitz or theming, and most offer good views of either the Fremont Street Experience or the desert. There's also a good, new pool. Sun–Thurs $39, Fri & Sat $69.

Four Queens Hotel & Casino 202 E Fremont St ☎702/385-4011 or 800/634-6045, ⓦwww.fourqueens.com. Glittery old-style casino, popular with Vegas veterans, which offers two towers of reasonably

tasteful rooms – some of which look right into the Fremont Street Experience – but little by way of diversions. Sun–Thurs $39, Fri & Sat $59.

Fremont Hotel & Casino 200 E Fremont St ☎702/385-3232 or 800/634-6182, ⓦwww.fremontcasino.com. Medium-sized casino in the heart of the Fremont Street Experience, where the spacious rooms have been refurbished to a high (if characterless) level of comfort, and one of downtown's best restaurants, the *Second Street Grill*, is just downstairs. Sun–Thurs $39, Fri & Sat $69.

Golden Gate Hotel and Casino 1 E Fremont St ☎702/385-1906 or 800/426-1906, ⓦwww.goldengatecasino.net. Founded in 1906, when Las Vegas itself was just a year old, the *Golden Gate* is the oldest joint in town. With 100 retro-furnished rooms, it's tiny by Vegas standards, and, if nothing else, slightly lower-key than its Fremont Street neighbors. Sun–Thurs $39, Fri & Sat $59.

The Golden Nugget Hotel & Casino 129 E Fremont St ☎702/386-8121 or 800/846-5336, ⓦwww.goldennugget .com. The first downtown casino to go for the luxury end of the market is undeniably glittery, and the rooms are certainly opulent, but if it's glamour you want it still makes more sense to stay on the Strip. Sun–Thurs $69, Fri & Sat $119.

Las Vegas USA Hostels 1322 E Fremont St ☎702/385-1150 or 800/550-8958, ⓦwww.usahostels.com. Former *Best Western* motel, in a slightly forbidding neighborhood six blocks east of the Fremont Street Experience, that's much the better of the city's two independent hostels, with dorm beds from $13 and private double rooms from $38. Rates include free pancake breakfast (cheap dinners are also available), and there's a heated swimming pool and jacuzzi, plus free pick-up from Greyhound. It's a short bus ride from the Downtown Transportation Center, with connections for the Strip, and the friendly staff can arrange city and national-park tours, including Limo Tours (with free champagne) to go clubbing.

Main Street Station 200 N Main St ☎702/387-1896 or 800/465-0711,

@www.mainstreetcasino.com. Downtown's best-value option, two short blocks north from Fremont Street, holds 400 large guestrooms plus a brewpub and an assortment of good restaurants. Just be sure to request a room on the south side, rather than right next to the freeway. Sun–Thurs $49, Fri & Sat $79.

Plaza Hotel & Casino 1 Main St
☏702/386-2110 or 800/634-6575,
@www.plazahotelcasino.com. The *Plaza* occupies one of Las Vegas's most historic locations, incorporating not only the spot where the first city lots were auctioned in 1905 but also the site of the former Amtrak station. Though it's tended to look somewhat run-down in recent years, the 1000-plus guestrooms have been refurbished to a surprisingly high standard. Sun–Thurs $39, Fri & Sat $49.

Sin City Hostel 1208 Las Vegas Blvd S
☏702/385-9955. This recently revamped independent hostel is located in a small, dilapidated former motel on the seedy fringes of downtown not far north of the *Stratosphere*. A dorm bed, or a basic "semi-private" double, costs $17.50; a slightly better double is $30. Demand is heavy, especially in summer, so reservations are required well ahead of time. Non-drivers won't enjoy walking in the immediate neighborhood, but the staff can fix up local tours.

West of the Strip

Gold Coast Hotel & Casino 4000 W Flamingo Rd ☏702/367-7111 or 888/402-6278, @www.goldcoastcasino .com. Old-fashioned, run-of-the-mill casino whose Western theme appeals most to older American travelers. The main selling point – unstated, of course – is that the much more upscale *Rio* and *Palms* casinos, with all their restaurants and other facilities (not to mention much pricier rooms), are both in easy walking distance. Sun–Thurs $49, Fri & Sat $69.

The Orleans Hotel & Casino 4500 W Tropicana Ave ☏702/365-7111 or 800/675-3267, @www.orleanscasino .com. Not a particularly exciting property to begin with, the *Orleans* is at a further

disadvantage by being located almost a mile off the Strip. However, the rates are not bad for such well-equipped rooms – many are L-shaped, with inglenook seating by the windows – and the on-site bowling alley and movie theater are plusses. Sun–Thurs $49, Fri & Sat $79.

The Palms 4321 W Flamingo Rd
☏702/942-7777 or 866/942-7777,
@www.palms.com. Although it's still among the hottest newer casinos in town, thanks to some very fancy nightclubs and restaurants and a consistently strong celebrity presence, the *Palms* is in many respects just a presentable but rather dull locals casino. Thus, while the rooms are very comfortable, you may not feel it's worth paying premium rates for the inconvenient location a mile west of the Strip. Sun–Thurs $79, Fri & Sat $129.

Rio Suite Hotel & Casino 3700 W Flamingo Rd ☏702/777-7777 or 888/752-9746, @www.playrio.com. While not nearly as fashionable as it used to be, the *Rio* still makes a reasonable attempt to rival the Strip giants. The restaurants, bars, and buffets are all excellent, the general theming isn't bad, the pool is great, and the rooms are large and luxurious, with floor-to-ceiling windows and great views – though most are not really suites, they just have sofas in one corner. However, the prices are not cheap, and whatever the *Rio* likes to pretend about its proximity to the action, the Strip stands a good half-mile away, along a highway no one would ever dream of walking. Sun–Thurs $109, Fri & Sat $159.

Texas Station 2101 Texas Star Lane
☏702/631-1000 or 800/654-8888,
@www.stationcasinos.com. *Texas Station*, a couple of miles northwest of downtown, is primarily a gambling joint for locals, but it's bright and friendly, with good restaurants and a movie theater, so staying in one of its 200 guestrooms is not a bad idea – assuming you have a car anyway. Mon–Thurs $49, Fri & Sat $89.

East of the Strip

Green Valley Ranch 2300 Paseo Verde Parkway, Henderson ☏702/782-9487 or

866/782-9487, ⓦ www.greenval
leyranchresort.com. The grandest of
the *Stations* chain of casinos, eight miles
southeast of the Strip, is a lavish resort and
spa, with 250 very upscale rooms that are
located well away from the casino floor and
aimed primarily at business travelers. It also
holds several good restaurants, and the
lavish *Whiskey* nightclub. Sun–Thurs $109,
Fri & Sat $169.

**Hard Rock Hotel & Casino 4475
Paradise Rd** ⓣ 702/693-5000 or
800/473-7625, ⓦ www.hardrockhotel
.com. The *Hard Rock* name has such a high
profile worldwide that if you didn't know Las
Vegas you might assume that "the world's
only rock'n'roll casino" is the best in town;
it isn't. Over a mile east of the Strip, it can't
match Las Vegas's showcase giants for size
or splendor. What the *Hard Rock* can offer,
however, is a relatively intimate and even
chic alternative, with guest rooms that are
well above average – the French windows
actually open – high-class restaurants,
a fabulous pool, and of course the odd
big-name rock gig. Sun–Thurs $99, Fri &
Sat $179.

**Las Vegas Hilton Hotel & Casino
3000 Paradise Rd** ⓣ 702/732-5111 or
800/732-7117, ⓦ www.lvhilton.com. The
Hilton is only a short way off the Strip – and
connected to it by Monorail – and its 3000-
plus rooms and suites are as plush as all
but the most expensive of its rivals. Still, it's
a rather sedate property that's monopolized
by conventioneers, and despite the big pool,
fun-seeking visitors are likely to feel that
they're missing out on the party. Sun–Thurs
$79, Fri & Sat $129.

**Motel 6 – Tropicana 195 E Tropicana
Ave** ⓣ 702/798-0728 or 800/466-8356.
Although comprising some 600 rooms, the
largest *Motel 6* in the country is much the
same as the rest – a low-rise straggle of
very routine lodgings. The location is good,
just ten minutes' walk off the Strip from the
MGM Grand – be aware that this is too far
to walk in summer, however – which may
well lead to it getting redeveloped shortly.
Sun–Thurs $35, Fri & Sat $59.

**Ritz-Carlton Lake Las Vegas 1610
Lake Las Vegas Parkway, Henderson**
ⓣ 702/567-4700 or 800/241-3333,
ⓦ www.ritzcarlton.com. Extremely luxurious resort in a gorgeous setting beside
the small, artificial Lake Las Vegas in
Henderson. It's not merely physically distant
from the Strip (roughly a half-hour's drive
away, there's a shuttle every 2 hours for
$30/day), but with its unhurried ambience
and style, the *Ritz-Carlton* is utterly unlike
any of the Strip resorts. Featuring lavish
spa facilities, and an Italianate "village" of
shops and restaurants, the *Ritz-Carlton* is
a destination in itself. Sun–Thurs $229, Fri
& Sat $259.

**Sam's Town Hotel & Gambling Hall
5111 Boulder Hwy** ⓣ 702/456-7777 or
800/634-6371, ⓦ www.samstownlv
.com. This casino, over six miles east of
the Strip, has made a determined and
largely successful effort to upgrade its
cowboy image, but remains primarily
popular with older visitors. The registration desk is in its large central atrium,
overlooked on all sides by 650 "Western-
themed" guest rooms that aren't nearly
as garish as that might sound. Sun–Thurs
$50, Fri & Sat $80.

**Sunset Station 1301 W Sunset
Rd, Henderson** ⓣ 702/547-7777 or
888/786-7389, ⓦ www.sunsetstation
.com. From its Spanish-mission facade
to the spacious, well-designed interior,
Sunset Station, opposite Henderson's huge
Galleria Mall, is the best locals casino in
the *Stations* chain. The rooms and pool
are good, and you're well poised for an
early-morning getaway to Arizona, but
really it's too far southeast of the Strip to
recommend wholeheartedly. Mon–Thurs
$60, Fri & Sat $90.

Super 8 4250 Koval Lane ⓣ 702/794-
0888 or 800/800-8000. The closest to
the Strip of Vegas's three *Super 8*s – a very
hot ten-minutes' walk in summer – offers
300 rooms, a pool, its own little casino,
and a reasonable restaurant. For dedicated
bargain hunters only. Sun–Thurs $42, Fri
& Sat $59.

Out of the City

**Mount Charleston Hotel Kyle Canyon
Rd** ⓣ 702/872-5500 or 800/794-3456,
ⓦ www.mtcharlestonhotel.com. The best

accommodation option in the Spring Mountains, thirty miles northwest of Las Vegas. Despite its somewhat forbidding facade, on the inside it resembles an old-fashioned national-park lodge, with lots of wooden furnishings, a high vaulted ceiling, a huge open fireplace, and an attractive sculpted tree with bronze leaves. Room rates vary according to which floor you stay on; the second floor costs $10 extra, the third $20 extra. Downstairs, there's a reasonably priced steak-and-seafood restaurant and an atmospheric bar. Mon–Thurs $79, Fri–Sun $109.

Mount Charleston Lodge Kyle Canyon Rd ☎702/872-5408 or 800/955-1314, ⓦwww.mtcharlestonlodge.com. A set of fancy, surprisingly comfortable log cabins, alongside a long-established but unexciting Southwestern restaurant high in the Spring Mountains, with views up to Charleston Peak. They're especially popular with honeymooners escaping Las Vegas. Mon–Thurs $125, Fri–Sun $175.

Essentials

Arrival

The quickest way for most people to get to Las Vegas is to fly there. It's easiest to drive to Vegas from Southern California, and buses connect to here from across the country. There is no longer Amtrak service to the city.

By air

The runways of Las Vegas's busy **McCarran International Airport** (☎702/261-5211, ⌨www.mccarran.com) start barely a mile east of the southern end of the Strip. However, the main terminal is a three-mile drive from the Strip via Tropicana Avenue and Paradise Road, while downtown is roughly four miles distant. Although some hotels run free airport shuttle buses for their guests, most people just hop in a **taxi**. Theoretically, a cab ride from the airport to the southern end of the Strip will cost $15 and up, and more like $25 for the northern Strip or downtown, but traffic delays can easily force those fares up by another $5 or so.

Car rental is readily available (see overleaf), while **Bell Trans** (☎ 702/739-7990, ⌨ www.bell-trans.com) run minibuses from the airport to the Strip ($4.75) and downtown ($6), leaving from just outside the terminal. Making the journey by **public bus** is possible, but slow and laborious; if you must, take CAT service #108 from the airport to the Stratosphere – where you can change to #301 for other Strip casinos – or take #109 to downtown (☎702/228-7433, ⌨www.catride.com).

By car

Easily the busiest driving route into Las Vegas is the **I-15** freeway from Southern California. Traffic congestion, especially close to the Nevada state line, means that the 269-mile drive from LA can take as long as eight hours. Las Vegas Boulevard South, which becomes the Strip, begins to parallel I-15 well before it reaches the city, but the quickest way to reach your final destination will almost certainly be to

stay on the interstate as long as possible. I-15 also connects Las Vegas with Salt Lake City, 421 miles northeast.

From the major cities of Arizona, direct access is provided by **US-93**, which leaves I-40 at Kingman, a hundred miles southeast. It joins US-95, running north from Needles, California, outside Boulder City; together, the two become I-515, which crosses I-15 immediately northwest of downtown Las Vegas.

The fastest way to get to Las Vegas from San Francisco is to take **I-80** and then pick up US-95 thirty miles east of Reno and follow that four hundred miles southeast to Vegas. However, threading cross-country via Yosemite and Death Valley national parks is a much more scenic option for the same drive.

By bus

Greyhound's long-distance buses to and from Los Angeles, Phoenix, Salt Lake City, Denver, Reno, San Diego, Bakersfield, and other cities use a terminal alongside the Plaza casino downtown at 200 S Main St. For schedules and fares, call ☎ 800/231-2222, or access ⌨ www .greyhound.com.

In addition, **Missing Link** run shuttle buses between Los Angeles and Las Vegas, with free hotel and hostel pick-ups (departs LA Mon, Wed, Fri & Sat; $42 one way, $79 return ☎ 800/209-8586, ⌨www.tmltours.com).

By rail

Amtrak stopped running passenger trains to Las Vegas in 1997, and its downtown terminal was demolished. Persistent rumor has it, however, that a new high-speed Amtrak service between Los Angeles and Las Vegas will come into operation at some point during the next few years, with a projected journey time of 5hr 30min. For Amtrak information, call ☎800/USA-RAIL, or access ⌨www .amtrak.com.

Getting around

If you're happy to see no more of Las Vegas than the Strip and perhaps downtown – and on a short visit, there's no great reason to venture any further – then it's perfectly possible to survive without a car. However, even the Strip is too long to explore comfortably on foot; walking more than a couple of blocks in summer is exhausting, so you can expect to make heavy use of taxis, shuttle buses, and the monorail links. Ranging further afield, the metropolitan area is very large and spread out, with only intermittent public transport access, making driving the only practical way to explore, while almost all the excursions detailed in Chapter 7 require the use of your own vehicle.

Driving

Las Vegas is plagued by severe traffic problems, especially on the Strip. That said, so long as you're not in a hurry, driving along the Strip is an exhilarating sensory blast, and worth experiencing both by day and night. When speed is a priority, use I-15, even for short hops. The fastest east–west route tends to be Desert Inn Road, which passes under the Strip and over I-15, with connections to neither.

Almost all the Strip casinos (except Bellagio) offer free **parking** to guests and non-guests alike, usually in huge garages at the back. The snag is that the walk from your car to wherever you actually want to go – your hotel room, for example – can be as much as a mile in places like Caesars Palace or the MGM Grand. If you're spending a day touring the Strip, it's probably best to go through the rigmarole of parking once only, preferably somewhere central. Valet parking, usually available at the main casino entrance, can save a lot of stress; it's nominally free, although a tip of around $2 is all but obligatory.

Renting a car is worth considering if you're either staying off the Strip or are planning on any amount of exploring. Typical rates in Las Vegas, including taxes, are $30 per day, $150 per week. All the major chains have outlets at the airport, and nearly every hotel is affiliated with at least one car rental outfit. Among the most ubiquitous are Hertz (☎ 800/654-3001, ⓦ www.hertz.com), Dollar (☎ 800/800-3665, ⓦ www.dollar.com), and Avis (☎ 800/230-4898, ⓦ www.avis.com).

Taxis

Every casino has a line of **taxis** waiting at its front entrance. Standard fares are $3 for the first mile and $1.80 for each additional mile, but the meter continues to run when you're caught in traffic. A $1.20 surcharge is added for trips to the airport; sample fares for the airport run are listed on p.169. **Tip** the driver between fifteen and twenty percent.

If you need to call a cab, try ABC (☎ 702/736-8444), Ace (☎ 702/736-8383), or Checker and Star (both ☎ 702/873-2000).

The Monorail

In 2004, the city finally unveiled the long-promised **Las Vegas Monorail** (daily 6am–2am; single trip $3, 10-ride pass $25; ☎ 702/699-8200, ⓦ www.lvmonorail.com), which runs along the eastern side of the Strip from the MGM Grand to the Sahara, making a business-traveler-friendly off-Strip detour via the Convention Center and the Hilton. Though the Monorail was trumpeted as the cure for local traffic problems, its repeated closures and limited range – it doesn't connect the Strip to either the airport or downtown, and won't be expanded anytime soon – make it more of a handy, high-priced extra than a much-needed lifeline. Also, for short hops along the Strip the Monorail can easily be slower than walking, because the actual stations

Sightseeing tours

Las Vegas is not a city that lends itself to organized **sightseeing tours**. On foot, you'd have to walk too far; on a bus, you couldn't visit the Strip casinos that are the main focus of interest. What bus tours there are tend to head out from the city instead, mainly to the destinations described in Chapter 7. Gray Line, for example, charge $42 for a seven-hour trip to Hoover Dam, and $39 for a seven-hour tour of Red Rock Canyon and Mount Charleston, though they do also offer a $39, five-hour tour of the Strip and downtown at night (☎702/384-1234, ⓦwww.grayline.com).

Operators running tours to the Grand Canyon are listed on p.153. Among them, helicopter companies such as Maverick (☎702/261-0007 or 888/261-4414, ⓦwww.maverickhelicopter.com) and Papillon (☎702/736-7243 or 888/635-7272, ⓦwww.papillon.com) also have scenic flights over Las Vegas itself.

tend to be located at the backs of the casinos.

There are also two **free monorail systems**, not connected with each other or the main line, that link Mandalay Bay with Excalibur via Luxor, and the Mirage with TI.

Buses and trolleys

CAT **buses** (☎702/228-7433, ⓦwww.catride.com) serve the entire city from their hub at the Downtown Transportation Center (daily 6am–10pm), a couple of blocks north of Fremont Street at Stewart Avenue and Casino Center Boulevard. Two routes, #301 and the express #302, run the length of the Strip and continue to downtown,

with service every ten minutes between 5.30am and 12.30am, and every fifteen minutes from 12.30am until 5.30am. The flat fare for these routes is $2. Buses in the rest of town operate between 5.30am and 1.30am only, for a flat fare of $1.25. A one-day pass, sold on board vehicles, costs $5, while monthly passes, available at the Downtown Transportation Center, cost $30.

Between 9.30am and 2am daily, the **Las Vegas Strip Trolley** (☎702/382-1404) plies the Strip between Mandalay Bay and the Sahara, calling also at the Hilton, for a flat fare of $1.65. Be aware that with both buses and trolleys on the Strip, due to heavy traffic, your progress over short distances may take longer than simply walking.

Information

Before departing on your trip, make sure to check the **website** of the Las Vegas Convention & Visitors Authority (ⓦwww.lasvegas24hours.com), as it's packed with information on lodging, activities, transportation, and tours, as well as loads of facts and figures about the city itself. (For more useful websites, see box overleaf.)

Although there is a **visitor center** at the vast Convention Center, 3150 Paradise Rd (daily 8am–5pm; ☎702/892-0711

or 877/VISIT-LV, ⓦwww.vegasfreedom.com), at half a mile east of the Strip it's too far to reach on foot, and its brochures hold little that you can't find more easily elsewhere. The casino where you're staying, for example, will almost certainly hold racks of brochures, and likely also has a booking desk that can make reservations for shows, tours, and the like.

Any number of **free sheets** and **magazines** provide local information in Las Vegas. The glossy magazines on the

Useful websites

ⓦ **www.gayvegas.com** The best source for information on the city's gay scene.

ⓦ **www.ilovevegas.com** Extensive listings and reviews from *What's On* magazine, plus an online reservation service.

ⓦ **www.lasvegasadvisor.com** This useful website contains user reviews of all the city's casinos and attractions, and issues a free weekly email newsletter. An annual subscription of $37 gives you access to such features as the busy forums on which members swap experiences of all aspects of visiting Las Vegas.

ⓦ **www.lasvegastaxi.com** Entertaining "inside scoop" from Las Vegas's taxi drivers, with an emphasis on nightlife. The huge "Hack Attack" forum holds a mass of personal opinions on hotels, shows, and just about everything else.

ⓦ **www.lvol.com** Information, reservations, and reviews for Las Vegas entertainment, including all the big shows.

ⓦ **www.lvrj.com** Website for the *Las Vegas Review-Journal*, with the latest details from the paper's *Neon* supplement and a searchable archive of every article for years.

brochure racks tend to consist largely of advertorial, but free newspapers like the *Las Vegas Weekly* and the *Las Vegas Mercury*, most readily available on the Strip in the Virgin store in the Forum (see p.97), hold useful reviews and listings. In addition, every issue of the daily newspaper *Las Vegas Review-Journal* has a four-page guide to the city.

Festivals and events

Las Vegas's annual calendar of events is most useful for planning when *not* to visit. While it has far fewer annual festivals than most American cities, Las Vegas does host several enormous conventions. Attracting up to 200,000 visitors, these can cause room rates to soar – partly due to the demand, but also because conventioneers tend not to gamble as much as tourists.

Early March
NASCAR Weekend/Winston Cup
☏ 800/644-4444, ⓦ www.lvms.com. The year's biggest racing event, held at the Las

Conventions to avoid

Mid-Jan Consumer Electronics Show
Mid-Feb Men's Apparel Guild (MAGIC) convention
End Feb Associated Surplus Dealers convention
Mid-March Construction Expo
Mid-April National Association of Broadcasters convention
Mid-Aug Associated Surplus Dealers convention (again)
Early Sept Men's Apparel Guild (MAGIC) convention (again)
Early Nov Specialty Equipment Manufacturers Association (SEMA) convention
Mid-Nov COMDEX computer show

Vegas Motor Speedway on Las Vegas Blvd north of downtown.

June

CineVegas ☎702/992-7979, ⓦwww .cinevegas.com. This young and still pretty small film festival is becoming more popular each year, with an increasingly impressive roster of films and a surprising number of A-list celebrities and filmmakers in attendance.

June to mid-July

World Series of Poker ⓦwww .worldseriesofpoker.com. Started at Binion's Horseshoe in 1970, the world's biggest gambling tournament is being held at the

Rio at the time of writing, with some $50 million in prize money offered in dozens of different events.

Early December

National Finals Rodeo ☎702/895-3900, ⓦwww.nfrexperience.com. Ten-day rodeo at Thomas & Mack Center – the rather characterless dome east of the Strip near UNLV – during which time casinos around town book plenty of country music acts.

December 31

New Year's Eve Major celebrations, festivities, and big-name, high-price concerts all over town.

Getting married

Perhaps the second most popular reason to visit Las Vegas – making your fortune being the first, of course – is to **get married**. Well over a hundred thousand weddings are performed here each year, many so informal that bride and groom just wind down the window of their car during the ceremony. Long before the Britney Spears fiasco, a Vegas wedding was a byword for tongue-in-cheek chic and partaken by many a celebrity couple (some of whose marriages actually lasted). What's surprising, however, is that in fact most marriages here are deeply formal affairs. Both the casinos and a horde of independent wedding chapels compete to offer elaborate ceremonies

with all the traditional trimmings, from white gowns and black limousines, to garters and boutonnieres.

You don't have to be a local resident or take a blood test to get wed in Las Vegas. Assuming you're both at least eighteen years old, carrying **picture ID**, and not already married, simply turn up at the Clark County Marriage Bureau, downtown at 200 S Third St (Mon–Thurs 8am–midnight, continuously from Fri 8am to Sun midnight; ☎702/445-4515, ⓦwww .accessclarkcounty.com/clerk/Marriage_ Information), and buy a **marriage license** for $55 cash. You can then walk over to the Clark County Court House at 309 S Third St (daily 8am–10pm), and

---

Casino chapels

Almost all of the major casinos have their own **wedding chapels**, which tend to eschew the kitschier elements so beloved by the independent chapels, and offer ceremonies starting at around $400. Among the most popular are:

Bellagio ☎702-791-7111
Excalibur ☎702-597-7777
The Flamingo ☎702-733-3232
New York–New York ☎702/740-6625
TI ☎702/894-7700
The Tropicana ☎702-798-3778
Wynn Las Vegas ☎702/770-7400

be married by the Commissioner for Civil Marriages.

If you want a little more ceremony than that, wedding chapels claim to charge as little as $55 for basic ceremonies, but at that sort of rate even the minister is an "extra," costing an additional $45, while you'll pay another $50 or more for photos. Count on paying at least $150 for the bare minimum, which is liable to be as romantic a process as checking in at a hotel and to take about as long. The full deluxe service ranges up to whatever you can afford.

In addition to the individual wedding chapels listed throughout this book, novelty options include plighting your troth on the deck of the *Enterprise* at the Hilton (☎ 702/697-8750); floating in a gondola in the Venetian's Grand Canal (☎ 702/414-4253); cavorting in medieval costume at Excalibur (☎ 702/597-7278); or beside your helicopter at the bottom of the Grand Canyon (Papillon; ☎ 702/736-7243).

Gambling

Although these days Las Vegas is about much more than just **gambling**, around ninety percent of visitors to the city still gamble, losing on average over $500 each. The basic choice lies between **table games** like blackjack or craps, played in the public gaze and surrounded by glamorous trimmings; **slot machines**, a more private pleasure in which the potential winnings are enormous, and you're spared the fear of not seeming *au fait* with the rules; and **sports betting**, with its hyped-up atmosphere and scope for proving that you know more than the bookies.

Despite Las Vegas's reputation as a stronghold of crime, the casinos simply don't need to cheat. Casino "games" are not so much games, where each player has the same chance of winning, as carefully structured business propositions, in which the casinos know that over time they are certain to end up ahead by virtue of their built-in "house edge."

As for **where to gamble**, that really depends on how you see gambling. If you think it's all about fun and glamour, then the Strip is the place to be, though the high minimum stakes at the largest casinos can mean you'll lose your money uncomfortably fast. If you feel that an authentic gambling hall should be gritty, grimy, and peopled by hard-bitten "characters," you may be happier downtown. If you see betting as a business, and want as much bang for your buck as possible, head instead for a locals casino, like the Stations chain, which tend to offer more generous odds at video poker and the like.

Your gambling budget

The generally accepted advice for visitors who want to experience the thrill of gambling while minimizing the risk is to never gamble more than you're prepared to lose. In addition, if you want to play for any length of time, don't bet more than around one-fiftieth of your total budget at any one moment. Thus if you've set aside $250 gambling money, it makes sense to play $5 slot machines, or bet with $5 roulette chips; if you've got $50, play with $1 stakes. Remember that even if the house edge on your chosen game is as low as two percent, that doesn't mean you'll lose two percent of your money and walk away with the remaining 98 percent. It means that if you play long enough, you'll almost certainly lose it all.

All Las Vegas casinos continue to ply gamblers, at both the slot machines and the gaming tables, with **free drinks** – just be sure to tip the waitress.

It's also important to point out that to gamble in Las Vegas, you must be **over 21** and have the ID to prove it; underage winners on the slots, for example, are not paid off. US citizens must pay tax on wins of $1200 or more.

Baccarat

Despite its sophisticated image, the card game **baccarat** – pronounced *bah-kah-rah* not *back-a-rat* – is a simple game of chance, requiring no skill. Up to fifteen gamblers can sit around the table, but only two hands are dealt. Although one is called the "player," and the other the "bank," you can bet on either. In each round, two cards are dealt to each hand. According to a complicated set of criteria, a third card may then be dealt to either hand or both, starting with the "player." All the cards worth ten points in other games – 10s, jacks, queens, and kings – are in baccarat worth nothing at all. Aces count as one, and other cards are worth their face value. The aim is for each hand to add up to as close to nine as possible; with totals of ten or more, the first digit is discarded. Thus a 4 and a 3 total seven; a jack and a 3 total three; and a queen, a 9 and a 4 also total three.

To bet, you don't need to understand why the third card is dealt or not. All you need to know is that only three bets are possible – "player," "bank," and "tie" – and that although successful "tie" bets pay off at 8 to 1, the house advantage of 14.4 percent on these means that they're never worth making. "Player" and "bank" both pay back even money, but a five percent commission is levied on successful "bank" bets. Even so, the lower house advantage (1.06 percent as opposed to 1.24 percent) makes betting on "bank" the better option.

Baccarat is traditionally offered by Strip casinos in high-roller enclaves with a minimum stake of at least $100. An all-but-identical, if faster-paced, version,

"mini-baccarat," is often played on the main casino floor, for lower stakes.

Blackjack

Las Vegas's most popular table game, **blackjack**, is also known as "21" in North America and "pontoon" in Europe. Although gamblers play against the casino, the dealer can't use any skill or judgment. What's more, the odds are relatively good to start with, while playing the mathematically "correct" way cuts the house advantage even lower.

Blackjack is played with a conventional 52-card pack. Each numbered card, from 2 to 10, is counted at its face value; jacks, queens, and kings are worth ten points; and aces are worth either one or eleven. Each player attempts to assemble a hand totaling as close as possible to, but not more than, **21**, while also being higher than, or equaling, the dealer's own hand. The best hand, an ace plus any card worth ten, is known as either a "natural" or a "blackjack."

Each round begins with each player placing their stake in their own betting area. All are then dealt two cards, face down, while the dealer receives one face down, and one face up. On your turn, you repeatedly choose whether to "hit," and be dealt another card face up. When you're ready to stop, you "stand" by pushing your cards, unexposed, beneath your stake. If your total exceeds 21, you're "bust"; turn your cards face up, and the dealer will take both cards and stake. If you're dealt a "natural," immediately turn over your cards. The dealer will then check his or her cards. If the dealer also has a natural, it's a tie (and the hand is over for everyone else); otherwise you're paid off at three-to-two odds.

After all the players have finished, the dealer plays his or her own hand, following set rules. When the dealer's final total is settled, the players' hands are revealed and the bets paid off. If you've beaten the dealer, you'll get double your original stake back, while you'll keep it if you've tied. A "natural" for the dealer beats any total of 21 using three or more cards.

ESSENTIALS

Gambling

The casino has a built-in advantage because you play before the dealer, and lose your stake for going "bust" whether or not the dealer also goes bust. The lure for serious gamblers is that by memorizing the cards as they are dealt, skilled players can consistently beat the house. Casinos minimize that threat by using several packs of cards at once, and shuffling at random intervals, but they also know that hardly anyone can count cards accurately in such noisy, stressful conditions. Some even distribute leaflets outlining the so-called "basic strategy," a chart that shows the "correct" response to every permutation of your own cards and the dealer's face-up card. In essence, this states that for totals between 12 and 16, you should stand if the dealer's face-up card is between 2 and 6, and hit if it isn't; if your total is 17 (other than an ace and a 6), stand; and always stand if your total is 18 or over.

The usual minimum stake for blackjack games on the Strip is $5, although it tends to rise in the evening at the larger casinos to $25. If you want to play for lower stakes, head either to the Sahara, for its $1 tables, or downtown.

Poker

In its traditional form, **poker** is unique in that gamblers play against each other, not the house. The casinos simply provide a room and a dealer, in return either for a percentage on every hand, or, less usually, charging by the hour. Playing poker against a bunch of total strangers is undeniably exciting, but it's not a risk to take lightly. While your opponents may not be cheats or crooks, they could well be professionals. The two most widely played variations, both of which offer scope for endless rounds of betting, are **Seven Card Stud**, in which each player is dealt two cards face down, four more face up, and then a final one face down, and **Texas Hold 'Em**, in which each player gets two face-down cards, and then five communal cards are dealt face up on the table. The object in both games is to make the highest hand possible using five of the seven cards.

Although casinos generally offer poker as a service for guests who will also gamble on other games, several have begun to stage poker tournaments, along the lines of the wildly successful **World Series of Poker**. The usual minimum bet on the Strip is $5, though you might find a $3 table.

Craps

The frenzied dice game of **craps** is the most intimidating casino game for novices. While it all happens too fast to learn by watching, it's not as hard as it looks, and you don't need to know all the rules to enjoy playing.

Craps is played on a baize table with high, padded walls. Although the players throw the dice, each game is operated by four casino employees: the "boxman," in overall charge; two dealers, who handle the bets; and the "stickman," who recovers and distributes the dice.

A different player is "shooter" in each game. The shooter lays a bet, on "PASS," and makes the "come-out roll" by throwing two dice. Meanwhile, the other players lay any bets they want to make, mainly on either PASS or "DON'T PASS."

If the come-out roll is 7 or 11, the shooter, and everyone else who has bet on PASS, wins immediately, while those who bet on DON'T PASS lose. Alternatively, if the come-out roll is "craps," meaning 2, 3, or 12, the shooter and all PASS bettors lose; DON'T PASS bettors win on 2 or 3, or retain their stake on 12.

A come-out roll of 4, 5, 6, 8, 9, or 10 becomes the "point". The shooter's sole aim is now to throw the point again before throwing a 7. If the shooter succeeds, PASS wins and DON'T PASS loses; if not, DON'T PASS wins, PASS loses.

After the come-out roll, anyone can also bet on either COME or DON'T COME. These are the same as PASS and DON'T PASS, in that the next throw becomes your "come number," and a COME bet wins if the shooter throws that number again before throwing a 7. If the shooter throws the point before either a 7 or the "come number," COME bets stay on the table.

After a come-out roll that's neither 7, 11, nor craps, anyone who has bet PASS/DON'T PASS or COME/DON'T COME can make an extra ODDS bet on that same bet. This time, you're betting that the relevant point or come number will or will not be thrown before a 7. These are the best-value bets in the casino, as they pay according to the precise likelihood of throwing that particular combination. Some casinos only allow ODDS bets up to double the original stake; others allow bets as much as a hundred times higher. For serious gamblers, ODDS bets are the prime reason to play craps.

Though the usual minimum stake for craps on the Strip is $5 or $10, the Sahara always offers $1 tables. The Stardust, Circus Circus, the Flamingo, and Excalibur are also renowned for low minimums, while it can be hard to find a table at Bellagio or Caesars that accepts stakes of less than $100.

Roulette

Roulette, a game of pure chance, revolves around guessing in which numbered compartment of a rotating wheel a ball released by the dealer will eventually rest. Players use the adjoining table to bet not only on the number, but also whether it is odd or even, or "black" or "red," or falls within various ranges.

All roulette wheels hold the numbers 1 to 36 – half red, half black – plus a green 0. Almost all in Las Vegas also feature a green 00. On this "double-zero" layout, the wheel has 38 compartments, so gamblers have a 1 in 38 chance of winning. When there's only one zero, the true odds are 1 in 37. However, the odds for successful bets are always set as if there were no zeroes. A correct number is paid off at 35 to 1, guessing the correct pair of numbers pays 17 to 1, and so on. Thus the zeroes give the house its advantage, and the double zero doubles that advantage to 5.26 percent.

Three strategies can improve your chances. The first is to play only single-zero tables. On the Strip, the Monte Carlo and the Stratosphere always offer single-zero games, though you may come across single-zero roulette elsewhere. The second is to avoid the bet that covers 0, 00, 1, 2, and 3, with its exceptionally poor odds of 5 to 1. The third is the most boring of all; the fewer spins you take part in, the better, so stake all you can afford to risk just once, on an (almost) even-money bet like red/black, or odd/even, and then walk away, win or lose.

Roulette ranks second only to blackjack for elaborate "systems". Most require you to keep doubling your stake on red or black until you win, and then stop. As you need a lot of cash to cover even a short sequence of losses, your initial stake can only be a small proportion of your total cash – but all you can ever win is that initial stake. As each game has a maximum bet, you can't keep doubling your stake anyway.

Slot machines

Thanks to glitzy new technology and highly competitive odds – not to mention huge jackpots – **slot machines** are more popular than ever. Where the house advantage on slots used to be around twenty percent, casinos these days (especially those at the lower end of the spectrum) vie to offer "looser" machines where their advantage is as little as five or even one percent. That's because gamblers are now prepared to invest higher stakes, staking $1 or even $5 a time rather than the old standard of 25¢. Note that you must be over 21 to play the slots, and have the ID to prove it; underage winners are not paid off. US citizens must pay tax on wins of $1200 or more.

Although modern slot machines still contain giant wheels decorated with different symbols – customers remain suspicious of machines that just show pictures of symbols on video screens – where the reels stop spinning is determined by microchips. Contrary to

Video poker

Video poker, the only video casino game to win widespread acceptance, is a cross between "five-card draw" poker and a conventional slot machine. Each time you play, five cards are "dealt" onto the screen. You can then, once only, be dealt replacements for as many of those five as you choose not to "hold." You don't need to know the rules of poker; the odds paid for all winning hands are listed on the machine.

slot-gamblers' lore, just because you hit a combination that looks close to a jackpot doesn't mean that you nearly hit the jackpot, and no sequence of combinations, or lack of winners, can indicate that a machine is "ready" to hit.

Beneath the surface glitter, there are basically two different types of machine. **Non-progressive** slots offer fixed paybacks for every winning combination, and in principle pay lower prizes, more frequently. **Progressive** slots, such as Megabucks or Quartermania, are linked into networks of similar machines, potentially covering the entire state of Nevada. The longer it takes before someone, somewhere, hits the jackpot, the higher that jackpot will be – digital displays show mounting totals that can run into millions of dollars.

All the major casinos operate slot clubs, which reward gamblers with points redeemable for discounts and upgrades, show tickets, or even cash. The value is never that high – at the MGM Grand, for example, inserting $2000 into the slots entitles you to $12.50 cash back – but it costs nothing to join, so if you plan to gamble for any length of time you might as well.

As for **where to play**, the slots are "loosest" (which is good) downtown, and anywhere locals play regularly, and notoriously "tight" at places like the airport or supermarkets, where most customers are just passing through. Strip options range from the Riviera, "where the nickel is king" and you can play for days on end, to the $500 machines in

the marble-walled High Limits room at Bellagio.

Sports betting

Nevada being the only state in the US where it's legal to place bets on the outcome of **sporting events**, almost every casino offers what's called a "Sports Book." In most instances it's a "Race and Sports Book," where you can bet on horseracing as well.

Although the odds for specific bets change minute by minute, almost all are set centrally, so there's little variation between individual casinos. Where you choose to gamble depends instead on what sort of atmosphere you prefer. Some Sports Books are high-tech extravaganzas, their walls taken up by vast electronic scoreboards interspersed with massive TV screens; during major sporting occasions, they're basically sports bars, filled by shrieking crowds. Prime examples include those at Caesars Palace, the Stardust, Mandalay Bay, and the Rio. Others, like the irresistible Race Book at the Imperial Palace, opt for a hushed, reverential ambience, giving each gambler a personal TV monitor, and hand-writing the odds with marker pens on white boards.

As for what you can bet on, the options are nearly limitless; not only can you wager on who will win pretty much any conceivable game, fight, or race, you can make more specialized bets, like predicting the combined points total in a game (referred to as the "over-under").

Directory

Banks and exchange Even with not a single bank on the Strip, there is still no easier city for getting cash or changing money: the casinos gladly convert almost any currency, day and night, and their walls are festooned with every conceivable ATM machine (most of which impose a service charge of around $2). Bear in mind that withdrawing cash with a credit card can incur punitive interest.

Disabled travelers While all the major casinos offer designated rooms for the physically challenged – plus, of course, accessible gaming facilities – the buildings themselves are on such a vast scale that visiting Las Vegas can be an exhausting experience. The Convention and Visitors Authority runs an advice line at ☎702/892-7525, and carries detailed information at ✆www.lasvegas24hrs.com; to arrange for a free disabled parking permit, call ☎702/229-6431.

Emergencies For police or medical assistance, call ☎911.

Gay and lesbian visitors While Las Vegas has long been a gay-friendly city, its tourist industry makes little provision for gays and lesbians, with no casino making any special efforts to attract gay visitors. Gay nightlife is largely a question of joining in with the local scene, with several gay bars and clubs located to the east and west of the Strip. If you're looking for something besides nightlife, there's the Big Horn Rodeo, which Nevada's Gay Rodeo Association (✆www.ngra.com) puts on each year in late April. For up-to-date information on events and happenings in the community, check out ✆www.gayvegas.com.

Golf For reservations at most of Las Vegas's forty or so golf courses, either check with your casino (most will help you to arrange a tee time), or contact Golf Reservations of Nevada (☎702/732-3119 or 800/627-4465, ✆www.golfvegas.com).

Hospitals There are 24hr emergency rooms at the University Medical Center, 1800 W Charleston Blvd (☎702/383-2000), and Sunrise Hospital, 3186 Maryland Parkway (☎702/731-8080).

Internet If you're traveling with a laptop, you should find it easy to connect from your room at normal hotel phone rates. In addition, most hotels offer in-room broadband connections at premium rates. You can also go online at Cyber Stop Internet Cafe, 3763 Las Vegas Blvd S (daily 7am–2.30am; ☎702/736-4782, ✆www.cyberstopinc.com), a better option than most casinos' business centers, which offer Internet access at ruinously high rates.

Kids Several casinos will look after your children while you gamble or simply explore; these include the various members of the Stations chain and also the MGM Grand, whose Youth Center costs $8.50 per hour for guests, or $10.50 for outsiders. Typically, you can leave your kids for a maximum of 3hr 30min in any 24hr period. For a babysitter, call Around The Clock Child Care (☎702/365-1040 or 800/798-6768).

Laundromats Laundry facilities are available in all hotels.

Library 1401 E Flamingo Rd (Mon–Thurs 9am–9pm, Fri & Sat 9am–5pm, Sun 1–5pm; ☎702/733-7810).

Medical For health problems not requiring a hospital, the independent, 24hr Nevada Resort Medical Center is located on the eighth floor of the Imperial Palace, 3535 Las Vegas Blvd S (☎702/893-6767).

Pharmacy CVS Pharmacy, on the Strip next to the Monte Carlo at 3758 Las Vegas Blvd S (☎702/262-9284), stays open 24hr daily.

Photography The only casinos in Las Vegas that allow visitors to take photographs of the action on their slot machines and gaming tables are Excalibur on the Strip, and the Four Queens downtown.

Post office While you should be able to mail postcards, letters, and packages from your hotel, the nearest post office to the Strip is behind the Stardust at 3100 Industrial Rd (Mon–Fri 8.30am–5pm).

Skiing Las Vegas Ski and Snowboard Resort, in Lee Canyon (☎702/385-2754, ✆www.skilasvegas.com), operates between late November and early April; they run a free shuttle bus from the city. Three chairlifts lead to ten different runs with a maximum vertical drop of 1000ft (daily 9am–4pm; lift passes $33/day). No accommodation on site.

Tax Nevada's sales tax is 7.25 percent. Room tax in Las Vegas is currently set at nine percent on the Strip, and eleven percent downtown.

Time Las Vegas is on Pacific Standard Time, which is three hours behind Eastern Standard Time and seven hours behind Greenwich Mean Time, but moves its clocks forward by one hour to operate daylight saving between the first Sunday in April and the last Sunday in October.

Tipping When in doubt, tip. The usual rate in restaurants or taxis is fifteen to twenty percent. In your hotel, for assistance with luggage, tip $1–2 per bag; for valet parking, $2; for maid service, $1–2 per day at the end of your stay; and for concrete help from a concierge, such as making a reservation, $5. You're also expected to tip dealers at the gaming tables a chip or two each time you win (and you can place bets on behalf of the dealer, if you choose). Bar staff, or cocktail waitresses bringing free drinks, normally expect $1–2 per drink.

Don't bury your head in the sand!

Take cover!
with Rough Guide Travel Insurance

Worldwide cover, for Rough Guide readers worldwide

Check the web at
www.roughguidesinsurance.com

UK: 0800 083 9507
US: 1-800 749-4922
Australia: 1 300 669 999
Worldwide: **(+44) 870 890 2843**

ROUGH GUIDES

Insurance organized by Columbus Direct. Columbus Direct are authorised and regulated by the Financial Services Authority. Columbus Direct, 41 Southgate, Chichester, West Sussex, PO19 1ET

small print & Index

SMALL PRINT

A Rough Guide to Rough Guides

Las Vegas DIRECTIONS is published by Rough Guides. The first *Rough Guide to Greece*, published in 1982, was a student scheme that became a publishing phenomenon. The immediate success of the book – with numerous reprints and a Thomas Cook prize short-listing – spawned a series that rapidly covered dozens of destinations. Rough Guides had a ready market among low-budget backpackers, but soon also acquired a much broader and older readership that relished Rough Guides' wit and inquisitiveness as much as their enthusiastic, critical approach. Everyone wants value for money, but not at any price. Rough Guides soon began supplementing the "rougher" information about hostels and low-budget listings with the kind of detail on restaurants and quality hotels that independent-minded visitors on any budget might expect, whether on business in New York or trekking in Thailand. These days the guides offer recommendations from shoestring to luxury and cover a large number of destinations around the globe, including almost every country in the Americas and Europe, more than half of Africa and most of Asia and Australasia. Rough Guides now publish:

• Travel guides to more than 200 worldwide destinations
• Dictionary phrasebooks to 22 major languages
• Maps printed on rip-proof and waterproof Polyart™ paper
• Music guides running the gamut from Opera to Elvis
• Reference books on topics as diverse as the Weather and Shakespeare
• World Music CDs in association with World Music Network

Visit www.roughguides.com to see our latest publications.

Publishing information

This 1st edition published October 2005 by **Rough Guides Ltd**, 80 Strand, London WC2R 0RL.
345 Hudson Street, 4th Floor, New York, NY 10014, USA.
14 Local Shopping Centre, Panchsheel Park, New Delhi 110017, India.

Distributed by the Penguin Group
Penguin Books Ltd, 80 Strand, London WC2R 0RL
Penguin Group (USA), 375 Hudson Street, NY 10014, USA
Penguin Group (Australia), 250 Camberwell Road, Camberwell, Victoria 3124, Australia
Penguin Group (Canada), 10 Alcorn Avenue, Toronto, ON M4V 1E4, Canada
Penguin Group (New Zealand), Cnr Rosedale and Airborne Roads, Albany, Auckland, New Zealand
Typeset in Bembo and Helvetica to an original design by Henry Iles.
Printed and bound in China by Leo

© Greg Ward 2005

No part of this book may be reproduced in any form without permission from the publisher except for the quotation of brief passages in reviews.
192pp includes index

A catalogue record for this book is available from the British Library

ISBN-13: 978-1-84353-478-5

ISBN-10: 1-84353-478-9

The publishers and authors have done their best to ensure the accuracy and currency of all the information in **Las Vegas DIRECTIONS**, however, they can accept no responsibility for any loss, injury, or inconvenience sustained by any traveler as a result of information or advice contained in the guide.

1 3 5 7 9 8 6 4 2

Help us update

We've gone to a lot of effort to ensure that the first edition of **Las Vegas DIRECTIONS** is accurate and up-to-date. However, things change – places get "discovered", opening hours are notoriously fickle, restaurants and rooms raise prices or lower standards. If you feel we've got it wrong or left something out, we'd like to know, and if you can remember the address, the price, the phone number, so much the better.
We'll credit all contributions, and send a copy of the next edition (or any other DIRECTIONS guide or Rough Guide if you prefer) for the best letters. Everyone who writes to us and isn't already a subscriber will receive a copy of our full-color thrice-yearly newsletter. Please mark letters: **"Las Vegas DIRECTIONS Update"** and send to: Rough Guides, 80 Strand, London WC2R 0RL, or Rough Guides, 4th Floor, 345 Hudson St, New York, NY 10014. Or send an email to **mail@roughguides.com**
Have your questions answered and tell others about your trip at **www.roughguides.atinfopop.com**

Rough Guide credits

Text editor: Chris Barsanti
Layout: Ajay Verma
Photography: Greg Ward, Demetrio Carrasco
Cartography: Rajesh Chhibber
Picture editor: Harriet Mills

Proofreader: Diane Margolis
Production: Julia Bovis
Design: Henry Iles
Cover design: Chloë Roberts

The author

Greg Ward is the author of the *Rough Guide to Hawaii*, as well as Rough Guides to Southwest USA, The Grand Canyon, Blues CDs, History of the USA, and Brittany and Normandy. He has also co-written guides to the USA and Online Travel.

Acknowledgments

Greg would like to thank above all Chris Barsanti, for his tremendous input in his swan song as editor; Sam, for making it good to be alive; and all those who helped in Las Vegas, including Christi Braginton and Stephanie Heller at Mirage, Martha Sandez at the Venetian, John McCoy at Cirque du Soleil, Sylke Neal-Finnegan at the Golden Nugget, Hylton and Robert at Papillon Helicopters; and Glenn Alai, Melissa Fields, Melissa Horacek, Amanda Keefer, Kris Lingle, Renee Rietgraf, Elizabeth Williams, Gina Yager, and Kristina Zemaitis.

Photo credits

p.80 MGM Mirage exterior © Courtesy of MGM MIRAGE

p.86 *Les Artistes Steakhouse* © 2005 Caesars Entertainment Inc

p.87 *Noodles* © Courtesy of MGM MIRAGE

p.92 Legends in Concert © Imperial Palace Hotel & Casino

p.95 *Mystère* © Tomasz Rossa/Costumes: Dominique Lemieux/2005 Cirque du Soleil Inc

p.109 *Avenue Q* © Jeff Christensen/Reuters/Corbis

p.126 Texas Station sign © DK Images/Demetrio Carrasco

p.128 *Dragon Sushi* © DK Images/Demetrio Carrasco

p.151 Valley of Fire © DK Images/Alan Keohane

p.152 Grand Canyon © DK Images/Demetrio Carrasco

Index

Maps are marked in color

INDEX

192